This Gallant Steelback

WILLIAM EWART BOULTER VC

Sergeant William Ewart Boulter VC photographed with his parents and fiancée together with local dignitaries at a public reception, in his honour, which took place at Wigston Magna, Leicestershire on 9 December 1916 (*Leicester Mercury*)

To Clive and Olive, with all good wishes, *Derek*

Derek Seaton

This book is dedicated to the memory of Sergeant (later Lieutenant) William Ewart Boulter VC and his comrades of the 6th and 7th Battalions, The Northamptonshire Regiment who fought in the great battles on the Western Front.

Contents

First published in 2010 by Derek Seaton, Leicester

Copyright © Derek Seaton 2010
ISBN 978-0-9528948-3-4

British Library Cataloguing in Publication Data
A catalogue record for this book is available from the British Library

Photographs: front cover - Sergeant William Ewart Boulter VC (Jeremy Birkett)
rear cover - William Ewart Boulter's VC group (By kind permission of The
Northamptonshire Regimental Association) (Derek Seaton)

By the same author:

Light amid the shadows

The Local Legacy of Thomas Cook

From Strength to Strength

From Tollgate to To Tramshed
(Helen Boynton and Derek Seaton)

A Tiger And A Fusilier

Leicester's Town Hall: A Victorian Jewel

*A Brief History of the Ancient Office of High
Bailiff of Leicester 1252-2005*

Designed by Birdhouse Design Limited 01530 837333

Printed by Abbotts Creative Print 01455 559986

Introduction

My interest in Sergeant William Ewart Boulter VC stems from the fact that he was born and raised in my home village of Wigston Magna, Leicestershire. I was always aware that a Wigstonian had been awarded the Victoria Cross, on the Western Front, in 1916 but other than that, I knew nothing of Billy Boulter. In 2008 I decided to undertake research into his life with a view to writing a biography of this gallant soldier.

It proved to be a fascinating journey of discovery and what emerged was the story of a remarkable and talented man. In many ways the First World War defined the direction of his life. The sheer hell of fighting on the Somme and actually surviving such an ordeal, where so many of his comrades died, was never far from his thoughts although he did not allow it to dominate his life.

He served in a Pals' Battalion, the 6th Northamptons, who distinguished themselves in the great battles on the Western Front where they won four Victoria Crosses. They were one of the battalions of the 18th (Eastern) Division commanded by the redoubtable Major-General (Frederick) Ivor Maxse, a tenacious trainer of men. As a division they excelled themselves and by the time they were disbanded, in March 1919, they had been awarded eleven Victoria Crosses - an outstanding achievement.

Billy Boulter was one of four brothers who went to war to serve their King and Country, remarkably all of them survived to return home after the cessation of hostilities.

Although the proud holder of the world's foremost decoration for gallantry, William Ewart Boulter kept his feet firmly on the ground and conducted himself, throughout the rest of his life, with modesty and dignity. My hope is that *This Gallant Steelback* will be seen as a fitting tribute to one of the heroes of that terrible conflict.

August 2010
Derek Seaton

Colour of the 6th (Service) Battalion, The Northamptonshire Regiment
(Reproduced by permission of the Northampton Chronicle & Echo)

Acknowledgements

My sincere thanks are extended to a great many people and organisations, who so kindly and generously contributed of their time and knowledge, without which it would not have been possible to publish *This Gallant Steelback*.

I am extremely grateful to the following:

Firstly, the family of William Ewart Boulter VC. His great-nephew Jeremy Birkett who gave me access to a wonderful collection of photographs, newspaper cuttings and memorabilia and willingly answered my many letters seeking information and clarification. His input was all important.

Ralph Boulter, a nephew, and his sister Mrs Marion Partridge together with another niece, Mrs Eileen Vann also made valuable contributions in enabling me to acquire information and family photographs particularly relating to Billy's brothers, George, Albert and Harold. Mrs Jennifer Crabtree, the great-niece of Rene and Billy Boulter, who kindly provided essential background details regarding her great-aunt.

Keith Perch, Editor of the *Leicester Mercury* for permission to use a number of photographs of William Boulter, Lynda Smart of the *Leicester Mercury* Library and to the *Mr Leicester* feature whose article on my research, led to contact being made with members of the Boulter family.

Peter Clarke, Assistant Editor of the *Northampton Chronicle & Echo* for permission to use some wonderful photographs from *The Northampton Independent* and *Northamptonshire and the Great War*.

To the many organisations who allowed me access to their archives and photographs, these included the British Library Newspapers, the Community History Network, Leicester City Council, the Co-operative College, Manchester, the Greater Wigston Historical Society, the Imperial War Museum, Leicestershire County Cricket Club, the Leicestershire and Rutland Family History Society, Malden Golf Club, Surrey, Merton Heritage & Local Studies Centre, the Midlands Co-operative Society Limited, the National Army Museum including access to the Canon W.M. Lummis VC files (held on behalf of the Military Historical Society), the National Portrait Gallery, the Northamptonshire Record Office, The Western Front Association (Northamptonshire Branch) Solo Syndication, London, Weston-super-Mare Library and the Wigston Civic Society.

I should also like to thank the many individuals who so kindly assisted me: David Belsham, Jon-Paul Carr, Northamptonshire Studies Manager, Northampton Central Library, Judy Faraday, Partnership Archivist, John Lewis Partnership, Reginald Maurice Gray, Didy Grahame OBE, MVO of the Victoria Cross and George Cross Association, Colin Hames, Dr Clive Harrison, Reg Holland, Derek Hunt, Tom Johnson, Colonel Robert Martin OBE, Dr Alastair Massie, the National Army Museum, Colonel Paul Oldfield, David Parish MBE, Andrea Pettingale, Librarian, Kettering Library, Peter Pitts, Paul Robinson, The Northamptonshire Regimental Museum, Joan Rowbottom, Brian Worth, Wendy Warren and Virginia Wright.

Three friends who gave me an enormous amount of assistance require special mention: Tricia Berry, Secretary of the Greater Wigston Historical Society, Adam Goodwin, Assistant Keeper (Archivist) of the Record Office for Leicestershire, Leicester and Rutland and Alderman Duncan Lucas the doyen of all things historical in Wigston Magna.

Finally I owe a huge debt of gratitude to Diane Batson who word processed the entire manuscript, Pamela Ward for scanning all the images onto her computer, Josie Bicker who meticulously proofread the manuscript and to Martin Bird for his skilful design work and layout of the book.

It only remains for me to say that if I have, inadvertently, omitted anyone from the acknowledgements who contributed to *This Gallant Steelback* please accept my apology. You can be assured of my gratitude.

Chapter One - Formative Years

By 1892 the ancient village of Wigston Magna, situated four miles to the south of Leicester, had experienced a rapid transition from a small rural community to an important industrialised township. It was served by the Leicestershire and Northamptonshire Union Canal at nearby Kilby Bridge and had railway links with Birmingham, London and the North.

Its very name Wigston gives a clear indication of its connection with the Danelaw and its earlier Scandinavian name of Viking's tun.

The first census of 1801 recorded a total of 1658 people residing in the village; ninety years later the population had reached 7013. Framework-knitting was introduced into the locality in the late 17th century and the industrialisation of a village, which could trace its roots back to the 6th century, was underway.

With the building of neighbouring South Wigston the area became (in terms of local authority status) an Urban District Council in 1894.

It was against this background that William Ewart Boulter was born at 51 Bull Head Street, Wigston Magna on 14 October 1892.

Fred (William Ewart's father 4 years), Martha (1 year) and five month old Albert.

Mary Ann Dore's family, over in Dunton Bassett, was recorded in the 1871 census and comprised of her mother Ruth and three older siblings. Ruth Dore (nee Hobley) was a native of Monks Kirby, Warwickshire, she was widowed in 1868 when her husband George, an agricultural labourer, died at the age of thirty-three years. The four children were Ann (16 years) a framework-knitter, George (11 years), Sarah (8 years) and finally Mary Ann then aged 6 years. The census showed a total of 496 people living in Dunton Bassett at that time.

Dunton Bassett Village School, now Dunton Bassett County Primary School (Derek Seaton)

Bull Head Street, Wigston Magna (Duncan Lucas)

His parents were Fred and Mary Ann Boulter. Fred was born in Wigston Magna on 2 August 1866 whilst Mary Ann Boulter (nee Dore) came from the tiny village of Dunton Bassett, four miles north of Lutterworth in Leicestershire, where she was born on Christmas Eve, 24 December 1864.

In 1871 the Boulter family was established in a worker's cottage in Bull Head Street and consisted of William and Mary Boulter and their five children - Alonzo (11 years), Harriett (9 years),

William Boulter's mother Mary attended the village school which was founded in 1849 by Thomas Stokes, a wealthy hosiery manufacturer of New Parks, Leicester, who was Mayor of Leicester in 1838 and 1841. He acquired a great deal of land in the Parish of Dunton Bassett where he was Lord of the Manor. A generous benefactor, he gave the land, had the school built and endowed it through the Stokes Charity. The school was enlarged in 1874.

Fred Boulter and Mary Ann Dore were married at the Independent Chapel in Long Street, Wigston Magna on 4 August 1890 by the Reverend T Cope Deeming. Fred's occupation was shown as a rotary hand and his wife was employed as a domestic servant.

The Independent Chapel was built in 1841 on the site of a former chapel founded in 1666. The

The former Independent Chapel, Wigston Magna, now the United Reformed Church (Derek Seaton)

second chapel was designed to seat 650 worshippers and was built at a cost of £1070. It later became the Wigston Magna Congregational Church.

The young couple's first child George was born on 31 October 1890 followed by William Ewart in October 1892. William's father's occupation was recorded, on his birth certificate, as a stocking framework-knitter. Fred Boulter had followed in his father's footsteps into the industry which, together with the manufacturing of boots and shoes, had firmly placed Leicestershire as an important centre of expanding productivity.

Fred Boulter was a supporter of the Liberal Party and, in particular, its redoubtable leader William Ewart Gladstone. In July 1892 Gladstone became Prime Minster for the fourth time (the only British politician to achieve this milestone), thus it was that the Boulter's second son became William Ewart Boulter.

Another local personality to be named after the Prime Minister was William Ewart Astill, the famous Leicestershire and England cricketer who was born at Ratby, in the county, in 1888.

Ewart Astill, as he became known, played for Leicestershire from 1906 to 1939 and, during those thirty-three remarkable years, he appeared on 628 occasions, the highest number of appearances in first class matches by any player in the club's history. He was the first professional captain of Leicestershire in the 1935 season and was selected to play for England in nine test matches between 1927 and 1930.

Fred and Mary Boulter's second son not only had the distinction of being named after William Ewart Gladstone he was also a "Woollyback." The hunting county of Leicestershire was famous for its lush pastures and fine grazing upon which

William Ewart Astill
Leicestershire and England
(Leicestershire County Cricket Club)

countless flocks of sheep grew and thrived. Their fleeces provided the wool for the local hosiery trade and natives of Leicestershire became known, far and wide, as "Woollybacks."

Further additions to the Boulter family came with the birth of Albert on 24 June 1894 and Harold on 14 July 1896. Finally a longed-for daughter Mabel was born in 1898 and then another girl Sarah May on 11 May 1904.

Mary Ann Boulter's involvement with the former Independent Chapel, by now the Wigston Magna Congregational Church, where she and Fred were married, grew as the years passed. In the church records she is shown, on the Roll of Church Members, as having been admitted in March 1899. The Baptismal Register records the third son Albert having been baptised in the church on 2 September 1894.

William's father was one of a group of hosiers in Wigston Magna who, on 6 May 1897, collectively took a bold decision to establish a pioneering venture in the township with the formation of the Wigston Hosiery Society. The aim was to promote an industrial Co-partnership. Initially, a number of men, in the locality, decided to start as factors only on a few pounds capital. A first-floor room, at the premises of the Wigston Working Men's Club in Long Street, was used as an office and warehouse. Helpful advice was given by Frank Ballard then managing a successful Co-partnership in Kettering.

Fred Boulter was elected to the first committee of the newly formed society which, by the end of 1898, had taken the decision to acquire workshops in a yard in Bull Head Street, at an rental of £8 per annum. The first Manager Alfred Wignall was appointed and new machinery was delivered to the premises.

The first factory of the Wigston Hosiery Society in Bull Head Street (Midlands Co-operative Society Limited)

Despite early problems the Wigston Hosiery Society steadily grew and gained a reputation for the production of good quality stockings which they sold exclusively to Co-operative Societies.

It was on 26 January 1899 at the Annual Meeting, that the Society after almost two years of preliminary negotiations, took the decision to enter into actual business operations. By 1901 the Society considered that the time had arrived for the firm to adopt a trade mark for their goods. Honesty and strong moral principles were the bywords of the business and they chose one word to describe their dealings – "Integrity."

*The Trade Mark Integrity
(Midlands Co-operative Society Limited)*

At the annual meeting of the Society, in February 1903, Fred Boulter was elected as Chairman of the Wigston Hosiery Society. That year also saw the appointment of the second Manager Mr C Smith.

Meanwhile the young William Boulter had commenced his education at Bell Street Infants' School situated in the heart of the community. Built in 1872, following the passing of Forster's Education Act 1870, the school was erected for 263 infants (average attendance 200).

*Bell Street Infants' School, Wigston Magna
(Duncan Lucas)*

The small building with the elegant bell tower was the village's first school to be built by the newly-created Wigston School Board. The Headmistress during the young Billy Boulter's time at the school was Miss Sarah Ann Abbott.

William, known to all his contemporaries as Billy, made many new friends. He was popular and well liked; team games and sporting activities he found particularly appealing and participated with relish. He duly moved on from the Infants' School to Great Wigston Board School in Long Street.

The senior school, which was opened in 1881, was built in local red brick and dressed with Ketton stone. The building was designed by the Leicester architects Robert Johnson and John Goodacre (R.J. & J. Goodacre), 5 Friar Lane, Leicester. The price of £3400 included the cost of the site. A local builder, Charles Eldridge Sharp of Bell Street, Wigston Magna was awarded the contract.

The building featured square-headed perpendicular windows, two chimneys and an attractive slender metal spire. When the school was formally opened on 18 October 1881 by Thomas

Great Wigston Board School, now the Record Office for Leicestershire, Leicester and Rutland (Derek Seaton)

Tertius Paget of Humberstone Hall, the Liberal Member of Parliament for the Leicestershire Southern Division, he described it as "that beautiful building."

It was here that the young Billy Boulter spent his formative years. He became renowned for his sporting prowess and was particularly successful at both association football and cricket. The school became the Long Street Council School in 1903 following the passing of the Balfour Education Act 1902 which resulted in the School Board system being replaced, as the providers of secondary education, by County Councils and County Borough Councils. The following year 1904, Billy left Long Street Council School aged twelve years.

Upon leaving school he commenced to work for the Wigston Co-operative Stores Ltd as a grocer's assistant in the village store.

In the meantime, the progress which had been achieved by the Wigston Hosiery Society, after early setbacks, indicated a steady and optimistic future which enabled the committee to consider the building of a new factory.

The committee, under the chairmanship of William's father Fred, purchased a plot of land in Paddock Street, Wigston Magna in 1905 and, by the following year, the Society's first purpose-built factory had been opened with new and up to date machinery installed.

The first factory in Paddock Street
(Midlands Co-operative Society Limited)

Fred Boulter's abilities and drive were tangibly recognised in early 1909 when, following the resignation of Mr C Smith, the Wigston Hosiery Society appointed him to the position of Factory Manager. He secured the post on merit following the advertising of the position and after three applicants had been interviewed by the committee.

Fred Boulter the Wigston Hosiery Society's third Manager (Midlands Co-operative Society Limited)

The steady progression by the head of the Boulter dynasty enabled him to improve the living accommodation for his growing family. By 1904 when Sarah May, the younger daughter, was born the family had moved from 51 Bull Head Street to a larger house in Welford Road, Wigston Magna and by the census of 1911 the Boulters were residing in a pleasant terraced house in nearby Harcourt Road.

Welford Road, Wigston Magna c.1906 (Duncan Lucas)

At this time the occupations of the Boulter children were as follows:-

George Boulter	Hosiery Operative
William E. Boulter	Grocer's Assistant
Albert Boulter	Boot & Shoe Operative
Harold Boulter	Boot & Shoe Operative
Mabel Boulter	Fancy Hosiery Learner

38 Harcourt Road, Wigston Magna. The home of the Boulter family in 1911 (Derek Seaton)

Sarah May Boulter was then aged six years and attending Bell Street Infants' School.

William's next move, in late 1911, was to join the Leicester Co-operative Society Ltd where he secured a position in the drapery department situated in the huge store in High Street, Leicester which was opened in 1884 and extended in 1904.

Part of the former Leicester Co-operative Society Ltd Store, High Street, Leicester (Derek Seaton)

The Wigston Hosiery Society's factory, ably managed by Fred Boulter, continued to make steady progress with advanced sales of its products. In 1911 orders had increased to a point where overtime had to be worked in order to keep up with customers' demands. By the end of that year the Society was able to announce record sales.

The former Independent Chapel, Long Street, Wigston Magna where the Boulter family worshipped. The gateway on the right is the entrance to Wigston Hall (Duncan Lucas)

Wigston Hosiery Society's second factory and offices in Paddock Street, Wigston Magna (Derek Seaton)

Such was the progress of the undertaking that the Society's Committee took the decision in 1913 for a "fine new building" to be erected in Paddock Street. This was only eight years since the decision had been made to relocate the business, in new premises, on their existing site. The plans were approved in April and tenders were invited from four firms. The lowest tender submitted by a building contractor, Mr Aldershaw, at £2214 18s 0d was accepted and the building of still further premises was commenced.

The premises of the Kettering Industrial Co-operative Society Ltd., Newland Street, Kettering (Peter Pitts)

During his father's creditable and progressive years William Boulter, in the furtherance of his own career, and whilst remaining in the employment of the Co-operative Society, had moved to Kettering in 1912 to take up a position with the Kettering Industrial Co-operative Society Ltd. He secured a position as an assistant at the Society's drapery department in Newland Street, Kettering.

Princes Street, Kettering (Derek Seaton)

He quickly settled into his new life in the pleasant Northamptonshire town and integrated

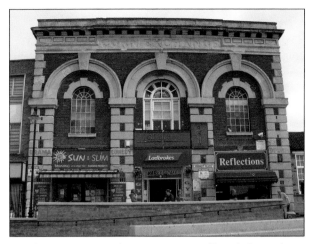

The former Corn Exchange, Kettering (Derek Seaton)

easily and fully into the local community. During his stay in Kettering he lodged with Henry and Elizabeth Shuffle at their home 38 Princes Street which was a short walk from his place of work in Newland Street.

The young sport loving Billy joined the Kettering Thursday Football Club where he quickly made a new circle of friends and became a popular player. He also became an enthusiastic member of the Old Adult School in the town. A good looking young man, with a pleasant personality, it was only a matter of time before he fell in love. The young lady in question was a Miss Florence May Lusher who, coincidentally, was born in Leicester in 1895. She was the fourth child and third daughter of Albert Edward Lusher and his wife Frances. Her father, a native of Norwich, had moved to Leicester to work prior to securing employment in Kettering. He was a wood last maker for the shoe trade and the family resided at 103 Kingsley Avenue, Kettering.

This was a happy phase in the life of young William Boulter. Enjoyable evenings were spent at the Palace Cinema housed in the former Corn Exchange in the Market Place. A splendid early Victorian building, the Corn Exchange was designed by the architect Francis Edmund Law of Northampton and erected in 1853 at a cost of £2,950. The upper floor, of the two storey building, was designed as the Kettering Town Hall.

Continuous nightly performances were available at the Palace Cinema and visits to "the Palace" were eagerly anticipated.

Life in many ways was idyllic and carefree as 1914 dawned but all was about to change as war clouds gathered across the skyline of Europe. Soon the lives of Billy and his young friends were to be changed forever.

Chapter Two - Woollyback To Steelback

The tranquillity of the English summer was shattered on Tuesday 4 August 1914 when it was announced that Britain had declared war on Germany. The First World War had begun and the world was to witness a titanic struggle for the next four years with horrific casualties, on an unimaginable scale, on both sides of the conflict.

The commencement of the Great War (as it was called from the onset) became unstoppable following the assassinations of the Archduke Franz Ferdinand the heir apparent to the Austro-Hungarian Empire and his wife, Sophie the Duchess of Hohenberg. The murders were carried out by a Bosnian Serb student Gavrilo Princip during the royal couple's visit to the Bosnian capital of Sarajevo on Sunday 28 June 1914. The immediate effect was the alignment and mobilization of the principal European powers. Austria-Hungary blamed Serbia for the assassinations. Russia, in turn, declared support for Serbia which led to Germany declaring war on Russia on 1 August and war with France on 3 August.

Germany mounted a swiftly planned attack on France which necessitated sending three armies through Belgium, this was known as the Schlieffen Plan. (Count Alfred von Schlieffen, Chief of the German Imperial General Staff 1891-1906).

The British Government acted without hesitation as Belgium was a long-term ally, protected by a treaty, and once that country's neutrality was violated Britain honoured its obligation and declared war on Germany.

On 11 August 1914, Field Marshall Earl Kitchener, the newly-appointed Secretary of State for War launched a massive recruitment campaign. Posters bearing the Field Marshall's stern picture, with finger pointing demanding: "Your Country Needs You" appeared everywhere. He called for 100,000 volunteers, aged between 19 and 30 years, and within three weeks his target was well exceeded. This initial intake formed the First New Army K1.

A month later, on 11 September, the formation of the Second New Army, known as K2, was authorised.

In Northamptonshire, along with every other county and city throughout Britain, young men flocked to the recruiting offices to answer the call of King and Country. William Boulter, along with six of his friends from the Kettering Thursday Football Club, enlisted in the town on 4 September 1914.

William Ewart Boulter 1914
(Leicester Mercury)

He was aged twenty-one years and eleven months on enlistment. His medical details were recorded as follows:

Height	5 feet 6¼ inches
Weight	131 lbs (9 stone 5 lbs)
Chest Measurements	35 inches girth when fully expanded 2¼ inches range of expansion

Private Boulter was allocated his service number – 14603 and posted the following day to the 6th (Service) Battalion, The Northamptonshire Regiment.

The Northamptonshire Regiment traced its origins back to the 48th Regiment of Foot which was raised in 1741 by Colonel James Cholmondley, as the 59th Regiment of Foot. In 1748 the Regiment was renumbered the 48th Regiment of Foot. The second component was the

58th Regiment of Foot which was raised by Colonel John Anstruther in 1755 as the 60th Regiment of Foot. This Regiment was renumbered as the 58th Foot in 1757.

The 58th Foot formed part of the besieged garrison of Gibraltar (1779-1783) by the French and Spanish forces and the gallant exploits of the 58th were gratefully acknowledged by His Majesty King George III and both Houses of Parliament. Permission was given for the arms of Gibraltar – a castle and key – to be borne upon the colours of the 58th and for the word Gibraltar to appear on the Regiment's cap badge.

In 1782, the 48th Foot was given the title "The Northamptonshire Regiment" and the 58th Foot became "The Rutlandshire Regiment" when regiments of the British Army were accorded county titles.

At the Battle of Talavera on 27/28 July 1809 the 48th was ordered by Sir Arthur Wellesley (created Duke of Wellington in 1814) to engage the French columns when they threatened to overwhelm the British positions. They fought with such ferocity and precision that the tide was turned and Wellesley was victorious. For its distinguished part in the battle the 48th was granted the Battle Honour Talavera and the right to include Talavera on its cap badge.

Under the Cardwell Reforms of the British Army, in 1881, the 48th and 58th were amalgamated to become the 1st and 2nd Battalions of The Northamptonshire Regiment respectively.

Cap badge of The Northamptonshire Regiment
(The Royal Anglian Regiment)

Thus Private William Boulter came to wear the distinctive badge of The Northamptonshire Regiment steeped in 173 years of tradition and service to the Crown.

The 6th (Service) Battalion was one of three Service Battalions (5th, 6th and 7th) raised by The Northamptonshire Regiment in response to Kitchener's recruitment campaign. Along with hundreds of newly-formed Service Battalions, throughout the country, they became known as Kitchener's Army or K's men.

The first Commanding Officer of the 6th Battalion was Lieutenant-Colonel George Eustace Ripley.

Colonel Ripley with three of his fellow officers of the 6th (Service) Battalion
left to right: Captain Wallace Willows, Lieut-Colonel G.E. Ripley, Captain
R.W. Beacham (Adjutant) and Captain Simpson
(Reproduced by permission of the Northampton Chronicle & Echo)

Colonel Ripley was born in 1864. He served with the 3rd Battalion, The Norfolk Regiment before joining The Northampton Regiment in 1889. He saw action in the Boer War where he was twice Mentioned in Despatches. Later he commanded the 4th Battalion (Territorial Force). At the age of 50 years, when he was enjoying country life with his wife and family at Cottingham, he offered to come out of retirement and to serve abroad. This true patriot, officer and gentleman was to have a profound influence on the young Private Boulter and the many hundreds of young soldiers who quickly grew to feel real affection and respect for their elderly Battalion Commander.

Initially the 6th (Service) Battalion, The Northamptonshire Regiment was stationed at Shorncliffe Camp, Cheriton in Kent where they became one of the units which comprised the 18th (Eastern) Division of the Second New Army; made up of men from the southern and eastern counties, under the command of Major-General (Frederick) Ivor Maxse. The Division which had three Brigades contained Service Battalions from thirteen Regiments as follows:

18th (Eastern) Division

53rd Brigade	54th Brigade	55th Brigade
8th Norfolk Regt	11th Royal Fusiliers (City of London Regt)	7th Queen's (Royal West Surrey Regt)
8th Suffolk Regt	7th Bedfordshire Regt	7th Buffs (East Kent Regt)
10th Essex Regt	6th Northamptonshire Regt	8th East Surrey Regt
6th Princess Charlotte of Wales's (Royal Berkshire Regt)	12th Duke of Cambridge's Own (Middlesex Regt)	7th Queen's Own (Royal West Kent Regt)

Pioneers: 8th Royal Sussex Regt.

In Major-General Maxse, the 18th Division had a charismatic commander who, following his commission in 1882, had served in the Royal Fusiliers before transferring to the Coldstream Guards in 1891. He had seen action at the Battle of Omdurman in the Sudan (1898) and had fought in the Boer War. He went on to become the Regimental Lieutenant-Colonel, Coldstream Guards and commanded the three Coldstream Battalions (1907-1910) from a small building in Wellington Barracks, London. In August 1914 he took the 1st (Guards) Brigade to France where he tasted reverses on the Western Front, in the early days of the conflict, at the Battle of the Aisne before returning home to take command of the 18th Division.

Major-General (Frederick) Ivor Maxse by George Charles Beresford in full dress as Lieutenant-General 1919 (National Portrait Gallery, London)

In Maxse, the 18th (Eastern) Division had a seasoned commander whose philosophy in relation to the fighting qualities of his troops centred entirely upon training. He believed, unreservedly, that thorough and intensive training was the key to success on the field of battle.

The divisional commander also realised the importance of getting to know his men and what was important to them as they prepared for battle. He quickly discovered that one of the most important NCOs in each of his battalions was the Master Cook! Training, feeding and explaining to his troops what was expected of them were the hallmarks of Major-General Maxse as the first commander of his new division of Kitchener's men.

The 6th (Service) Battalion of the Northamptonshire Regiment settled down to a rigorous training programme in their camp at Colchester and one who quickly found his feet and adapted with ease into the military way of life was Private Boulter. He soon emerged as a competent soldier, who could master the various weapons of an infantryman and displayed leadership qualities which quickly put him in line for promotion.

An enthusiastic and talented sportsman he was also involved, whenever the opportunity presented itself, in sporting activities and represented his battalion on the football field. His all-round abilities as a soldier soon caught the discerning eye of Lieutenant-Colonel Ripley and steady progress through the ranks was assured.

Throughout twelve months of intensive training at Shorncliffe, Colchester and at Codford St Mary on Salisbury Plain, to prepare the battalion for the Western Front, William Boulter's service record makes interesting reading:

Rank	Date
Attested Private	4 September 1914
Appointed (paid) Lance Corporal	29 September 1914
Promoted Corporal	18 November 1914
Appointed (paid) Lance Sergeant	13 April 1915

During this time he excelled as a corporal in the Machine Gun Detachment of the 6th Battalion, under Sergeant George Sismey, before developing additional skills as a bomber. At the commencement of the war, the British Army was in the process of experimenting to develop an effective hand-grenade. A variety of prototype bombs were used, initially on the Western Front, but it wasn't until 1915 that a superior type grenade – the Mills Bomb (No 5) was introduced.

The forerunner to the Mills Bomb was developed in Belgium but it possessed a suspect firing mechanism. It was the British born engineer William Mills who, having opened a munitions factory in Birmingham for making hand grenades, together with specialist colleagues significantly improved the weapon in terms of safety and reliability.

The Mills Bomb (No 5) was introduced on the Western Front in the spring of 1915 and by July 1916 was being manufactured and supplied in vast quantities to the British Army. The oval-shaped bomb, which weighed 1½ lbs, was a powerful short-range weapon much admired and feared by the German infantrymen who lacked a similar bomb with such devastating capabilities. A trained bomber would carry his consignment of grenades either in a 10-pocket 'waistcoat' carrier or in a canvas bag or bucket.

The specialist skills of a bomber centred upon the soldier's ability to throw the grenade swiftly and accurately over a distance of some forty yards. Sportsmen such as Sergeant Boulter were able to use their masterly throwing of a cricket ball, which involved a similar technique, to great effect. Grenade throwers became an essential element of the attacking British infantrymen and, deservedly, earned the right to wear a specialist badge to denote their skills and level of achievement. The badge was in the form of a grenade with a scarlet flame and was proudly worn on the right upper-arm.

William Mills was knighted in 1922 for his wartime services.

During his first twelve months of service, Sergeant Boulter had become an accomplished soldier and a respected comrade within the ranks of the sturdy men of Northamptonshire. Their unique nickname "The Steelbacks" originated from the 2nd Battalion's legendary ability to take their floggings. This brutal punishment was abolished in the British Army in 1881 but the nickname was proudly retained.

Sergeant William Ewart Boulter, 6th (Service) Battalion (Leicester Mercury)

Despite his successful progression through the ranks and his skill as a bomber it was achieved, somewhat surprisingly, against a background of misdemeanours which resulted in him appearing before his Company Commander (C Company) on a number of unexpected charges. Entries on his Company Conduct Sheet all centred on his bizarre and unacceptable levels of time keeping:

Accused
Lance-Corporal W.E. Boulter

Place
Colchester

Date
1 November 1914

Charge
Absent off Pass from 12.00 midnight on 1 November until 12.00 noon on 2 November (12 hours)

Award
Admonished. Forfeits 1 day's pay by Royal Warrant

Accused
Corporal W.E. Boulter

Place
Colchester

Date
23 March 1915

Charge
Absent from 5.55pm Parade

Award
Reprimanded

Accused
Corporal W.E. Boulter

Place
Codford

Date
5 July 1915

Charge
Absent off Pass from 9.00pm 5 July 1915 until 12.15 noon 6 July 1915 (15 hours 15 minutes)

Award
Reprimanded. Forfeits 2 days pay by Royal Warrant

In view of this poor disciplinary record one can only conclude that his rapid promotion, through the ranks, resulted from his excellent performances as an infantryman and his skills of leadership. This, undoubtedly, led to a judgement by his superiors that, when he was needed most on the battlefield, he would not be found wanting. This assessment was to be prophetic indeed.

Lance-Sergeant Boulter's popularity amongst the rank and file of the 6th Battalion was considerable, he made friends easily and he possessed a positive attitude allied to a sense of humour. Perhaps he was well liked because he too could "land himself in trouble" from time to time, as many soldiers did, but he accepted his punishment and was a survivor.

The 6th (Service) Battalion, The Northamptonshire Regiment on parade before departure for France (Reproduced by permission of the Northampton Chronicle & Echo)

On 26 June 1915 King George V came to inspect the 18th (Eastern Division) followed by a march past, which took place near to Stonehenge. The presence of the King to take the salute of Major-General Maxse's well-drilled and intensely trained division was a sure sign to all that embarkation to the Western Front was imminent.

The 18th Division finally left for France on 25 July 1915. The 6th Battalion, The Northamptonshire Regiment, departed from their camp at Codford St Mary and proceeded to Warminster where they were moved by train to Southampton to board their troopship which landed in Bolougne on the following day.

Upon arrival in France the units of the 18th Division assembled to join X Corps of the newly formed Third Army commanded by General Sir Charles Monro.

Action was first encountered during August when the 18th Division took over part of the front-line in the Somme area and was engaged in a sector which included Carnoy and Marmetz. There was little intensive fighting, in the division's allocated area at this particular time, thus the new battalions were able to acclimatise gradually and to gain in confidence in their early days in the trenches. This enabled Major-General Maxse to concentrate upon developing additional stages of his training programme to equip the 18th Division for the battles which lay ahead.

Meanwhile Lance-Sergeant Boulter was continuing to enjoy mixed fortunes. On 26 July 1915 he was promoted to the rank of Sergeant but three months later he again found himself in trouble, on this occasion he had to appear before his Commanding Officer on the following charge:

The boot repairers, in camp, prepare the men of the 6th Northamptons for action (Reproduced by permission of the Northampton Chronicle & Echo)

Accused
Sergeant W.E. Boulter

Place
In the Field

Date
24 October 1915

Charge
Late on Church Parade

Witness
R.S.M. F.Fulcher

Award
Reprimanded

Awarded by
Lieutenant-Colonel G.E. Ripley
Commanding Officer

Reporting late on a Battalion Church Parade was a serious offence and, whatever the reason, Sergeant Boulter's absence was immediately noticed by his eagle-eyed Regimental Sergeant-Major (Warrant Officer Class I) R.S.M. Frederick Fulcher. Clearly, on this occasion, when his non-appearance, at the appointed time, led to the involvement of both his Commanding Officer and the Regimental Sergeant Major, the most senior NCO in the unit, Sergeant Boulter's disciplinary lapses were becoming a matter of some concern. He must have concluded, after this latest episode, that patience was running thin and that he could not afford to step out of line again. This incident appears to have taught him a salutary lesson – no more charges followed.

The first winter to be encountered by the 18th Division on the Western Front saw the units holding the Fricourt sector in the Somme area. The 6th Battalion, The Northamptonshire Regiment spend Christmas in the trenches near to Fricourt.

Men of the 6th (Service) Battalion, The Northamptonshire Regiment experiencing the harsh realities of life in the frozen trenches (Reproduced by permission of the Northampton Chronicle & Echo)

On 19 December 1915 a major change at the top of the British High Command was announced. Field Marshall Sir John French was replaced by General Sir Douglas Haig, GOC First Army, as Commander-in-Chief of the British Expeditionary Force. As 1915 drew to a close, plans were being prepared for a new joint offensive by the British and French Armies on the Western Front.

Expansion of the British Army led to the creation of a new Fourth Army which was formed on 5 February 1916 under the command of Lieutenant-General Sir Henry Rawlinson.

An experienced corps commander, Rawlinson had commanded IV Corps in Haig's First Army at Neuve Chapelle, Aubers Ridge and Loos. As a newly promoted army commander Rawlinson was given responsibility for mounting a major campaign that would forever be remembered as the Battle of the Somme. The Fourth Army was composed mainly of recruits into the service battalions who had been trained in the United Kingdom and France in readiness for action on the Western Front. They were now to undergo five months of intensive training specifically for the forthcoming offensive at the Somme.

Preparations intensified during the spring of 1916 and, on 1 March, the 18th (Eastern) Division joined XIII Corps of the new Fourth Army. The corps commander was Lieutenant-General Walter Norris Congreve VC. As a Captain in The Rifle Brigade (Prince Consort's Own) he had been awarded the Victoria Cross in the Boer War. He now had responsibility for a potentially formidable fighting force waiting to be tested in a major battle.

The 6th Battalion, The Northamptonshires, spent the first three months of 1916 tidying up their sector which they duly handed over before moving to the Bray area. On a cold winter's day, whilst surveying the line, the Commanding Officer Lieutenant-Colonel Ripley and the battalion's Adjutant, Captain R.W. Beacham were wounded following the explosion of a nearby stray shell. The colonel was invalided back to his home in Northamptonshire. As he recovered from his wounds, efforts were made to persuade him to remain in England and to take up an important home-based appointment. He steadfastly refused and insisted upon returning to France in order to lead "my boys" in their first big offensive.

Whenever the 6th Battalion was not in action or involved in training exercises, Sergeant Boulter continued his sporting activities at every available opportunity. His friend Sergeant George Sismey described him, graphically, in the following terms: "A man of medium height, strong and well-built and full of spirit. He was a good footballer and played as a forward for the battalion in France."

Throughout March and April 1916, the 18th

(Eastern) Division successfully held the Carnoy sector. The 6th Battalion, The Northamptonshire Regiment, really had cause to celebrate, when on 24 April, Lieutenant-Colonel Ripley returned from his period of convalescence in England. Spirits were lifted significantly as the commanding officer reappeared to take charge of his beloved 6th "Steelbacks" once more.

During this time Major-General Maxse was a regular visitor to the thirteen battalions which made up the 18th (Eastern) Division. Little escaped his notice or intervention as he sought to rigorously train, equip, strengthen and maximise the fighting qualities of his soldiers for the great conflict which lay ahead.

As the units spent all their available time seeking to achieve a state of readiness another remarkable soldier joined the 18th (Eastern) Division. During

May, Lieutenant-Colonel Francis Aylmer Maxwell VC was appointed to be the new Commanding Officer of the 12th (Service) Battalion of The Duke of Cambridge's Own (Middlesex Regiment) in the 54th Brigade.

Having joined the Indian Staff Corps in November 1893, Frank Maxwell, as he was known to his fellow officers, had enjoyed a brilliant military career. He was created a Companion of the Distinguished Service Order *(The London Gazette* 20 May 1898*)*, the insignia was presented to him by Queen Victoria, at Windsor Castle on 25 June 1898. He served in South Africa with Roberts's Light Horse and was, for a time, ADC (aide-de-camp) to Lord Kitchener, Commander-in-Chief, British Forces.

On 8 March 1901, Lieutenant Maxwell was awarded the Victoria Cross. His citation read as follows:

Lieutenant Francis Aylmer Maxwell
Indian Staff Corps, attached to Roberts's Light Horse

On 31 March 1900 at Korn Spruit, South Africa, Lieutenant Maxwell carried out the self-imposed duty of saving the guns. He went out on five different occasions and assisted in bringing in two guns and three limbers, one of which he, Captain Humphreys and some gunners dragged in by hand. He also went out with Captain Humphreys and Lieutenant Stirling to try to get the last gun in, and remained there until the attempt was abandoned. During a previous campaign (the Chitral Expedition 1895) he had removed the body of Lieutenant-Colonel F.D. Battye, Corps of Guides, under fire for which, though recommended, he received no award.

Lieutenant Maxwell became a Captain in the Indian Army in July 1901 and, the following year, he was appointed ADC, once again, to Lord Kitchener, the Commander-in-Chief, East Indies. He went on to serve as a Brigade-Major in the Indian Army and as a Major in the Australian Commonwealth Military forces. Francis Maxwell was promoted to Brevet Lieutenant-Colonel on 29 November 1915.

He was a member of the Viceroy's staff in India prior to being posted to command the 12th (Service) Battalion, The Middlesex Regiment at the age of 44 years.

Sergeant William Boulter was soon to meet this

ferocious and gallant officer. Their joint impact upon events was destined to ensure that the achievements of the 18th (Eastern) Division were to go down in the annals of military history.

Cap badge of The Middlesex Regiment.

Lieutenant-Colonel Francis Aylmer Maxwell, VC, DSO (1912) (National Army Museum)

Chapter Three - This Gallant Act

The Battle of the Somme began on 1 July 1916. The British Army took the leading role in the new campaign supported by the French Army, whose forces were still heavily involved in the costly Battle of Verdun, which had commenced on 21 February 1916.

An intensive British artillery bombardment was launched on 24 June. The continuous shelling was designed to effect the cutting of the barbed wire, which protected the German positions, and to destroy the enemy's trench system. The successful outcome of this concentrated barrage was

preparations were complete, it was now the eve of the first major offensive to be fought by "The Steelbacks."

As they anxiously awaited the dawn and the order to advance, all ranks of the 6th Battalion received an unexpected gift from their Commanding Officer prior to going 'over the top'. Every soldier was given a personal gift of a hard-boiled egg from Lieutenant-Colonel Ripley. All were touched by this simple act of kindness which demonstrated to them, at that most critical moment, the affection and thoughtfulness of Colonel Ripley

Officers of the 6th (Service) Battalion, The Northamptonshire Regiment prior to the battalion's first major battle (Reproduced by permission of the Northampton Chronicle & Echo)

considered to be crucial in paving the way for the great breakthrough by units of the Allied infantry one week later.

The greater burden of responsibility rested with General Sir Henry Rawlinson whose Fourth Army provided twelve divisions supported by two divisions of General Sir Edmund Allenby's Third Army to the north and two divisions of the powerful XX Corps of the French Sixth Army, commanded by General Emile Fayolle, on the southern flank. Facing them was the formidable well-entrenched German Second Army under their Prussian commander, General Fritz von Below.

The 6th (Service) Battalion, The Northamptonshire Regiment assembled in their forward trenches along with their comrades of the other participating battalions of the 18th (Eastern) Division under the command of Major-General Ivor Maxse. The training was over, the

for each and every one of them.

As the whistles sounded zero hour, at 7.30am, the infantrymen left their trenches in continuous waves along a 25 mile front to attack the German positions. By nightfall the British casualties had reached catastrophic levels of 57,470 officers and men, of which 19,240 had been killed. The day would be forever remembered as the bloodiest day in the history of the British Army.

The artillery bombardment had failed to break the German wire to any significant degree and many of the well established enemy dugouts had escaped largely intact. Added to which the German artillery remained a potent force. The advancing lines of British infantry had little chance against the accurate and tenacious fire of the German machine-gun crews.

Few gains were made by the attacking Allied Forces. The British XIII Corps however made significant progress and its 18th Division achieved all of its planned objectives on day one. By mid-afternoon on 1 July the division had taken each of the German positions assigned to them and the Northamptonshires had played a crucial role in this breakthrough. The division took part in the assault on the German front line, north of Carnoy and successfully captured Montauban Ridge and village, Pommiers Redoubt, Caterpillar Wood and Marlborough Wood.

It was the taking of the Pommiers Redoubt where "The Steelbacks", supporting the two attacking units, the 11th Royal Fusiliers and the 7th Bedfordshire Regiment, achieved their initial success. In the attack they sustained heavy casualties and deservedly won the unrestrained admiration of their Commanding Officer.

In a letter to William Henry Holloway, the Editor of *The Northampton Independent* Lieutenant-Colonel Ripley wrote: "I am more than proud of my men. They advanced through a heavy barrage of artillery fire as steadily as if on parade and straight to their allotted objectives, where they worked like Trojans amidst a heavy bombardment."

The 6th Battalion's losses on the first day of the Battle of the Somme	
Killed	29
Wounded	126
Missing	4
Shell Shock	1
Total casualties	**160**

For the next twelve days the 6th Northamptons consolidated the positions which they had taken during the attack. On 7 July a congratulatory message was received from His Majesty King George V by the Commander-in-Chief, General Sir Douglas Haig. The following day the communication, which was conveyed to unit commanders, was relayed to the Officers, NCOs and men of the 6th Battalion. The message from The King read as follows:-

"Please convey to the Army under your command my sincere congratulations on the results achieved in the recent fighting.
I am proud of my troops -
none could have fought more bravely."

On 9 July the 6th Battalion moved into camp at Bois des Tailles prior to a visit, the following day, by their Divisional Commander, Major-General Ivor Maxse. Was this visit designed to congratulate "The Steelbacks" upon their recent successes or had the General another objective in his sights for the redoubtable men of Northamptonshire? All was to be revealed with no lack of haste.

The British High Command had decided upon a bold plan to launch an attack on the German second line defences situated to the south of the British front. The attack scheduled to take place five days later, on a four mile frontage, was designed to advance in a north-easterly direction from Fricourt and Mametz. The strategic objective was the Bazentin Ridge and involved taking the villages of Bazentin-le-Petit, Bazentin-le-Grand and Longueval together with a number of heavily defended woods in the path of the advance.

The plan for this daring attack was put forward by General Rawlinson in which he proposed to use four divisions in a surprise dawn offensive. Despite Rawlinson's confidence and optimism, General Haig had severe reservations about the plan. He was concerned that a mass concentration of troops was to be assembled during the hours of darkness. Haig also had to be convinced that the infantrymen had been adequately trained to undertake this dangerous mission. Corps and divisional commanders threw their weight behind the plan and made known their support of General Rawlinson's proposed attack to the Commander-in-Chief.

Despite his lack of enthusiasm for Rawlinson's proposals nevertheless General Haig gave the plan his approval and sanctioned its implementation.

The four divisions, chosen by General Rawlinson, for the attack were, from left to right, the 21st and 7th Divisions of XV Corps and the 3rd and 9th Divisions of XIII Corps of the Fourth Army.

In addition to the main thrust of the attack, a single and strategic objective was allocated to Major General Maxse's 18th Division. This was the taking and holding of Trones Wood which occupied a critical position on the extreme right of the attacking force. It was vitally important that the wood was captured, in its entirety, in order to protect the right flank of General Rawlinson's attacking four divisions. The exposure of the advancing infantrymen to a heavily defended Trones Wood had the potential to produce enormous casualties and threaten the success of the entire operation.

The area to the north of the River Somme sector contained a number of woods largely held by the enemy. Often referred to by military historians as 'The Horseshoe of Woods' they were comprised of Mamtz Wood, the Bazentin Woods, High Wood, Delville Wood, Bernafay Wood and Trones Wood. Each of the woods presented a difficult challenge to attacking forces, none more so than Trones Wood. Sergeant William Ewart Boulter was about to meet his moment of destiny.

Trones Wood had changed hands on a number of occasions immediately prior to the mounting attack planned for Friday 14 July. Units of the 30th Division of XIII Corps, commanded by Major-General John Stuart Mackenzie Shea, had regained the wood on 11 July but the following day the enemy had retaken it with the exception of a small area at the southern end.

On 12 July Major-General Maxse received orders from Lieutenant-General Walter Norris Congreve VC, his Corps Commander, that the 18th Division was to relieve the exhausted 30th Division who had fought to a standstill. In addition, the 18th Division was ordered to recapture Trones Wood **at all costs** and that this objective must be achieved by midnight on 13 July. Meanwhile, on the eve of the battle, the German High Command appointed General Max von Gallwitz to command their Second Army in place of General Below.

The attack on Trones Wood

Major-General Maxse immediately effected the relief of the battered 30th Division which the 18th Division completed by 10.00am on 13 July. He then proceeded to detail his 55th Brigade, under the command of Brigadier-General Sir Thomas Jackson, to recapture the entire wood. Failure could not be contemplated.

In order to strengthen the attacking 55th Brigade, Major-General Maxse placed the 12th (Service) Battalion, The Middlesex Regiment and the 6th (Service) Battalion, The Northamptonshire Regiment, both of the 54th Brigade, at the disposal of Brigadier-General Jackson as additional back-up battalions if they should be required.

As eventide descended on Trones Wood, the decision was taken, by the divisional commander, to retain Lieutenant-Colonel Ripley as liaison officer at the 54th Brigade Headquarters. Major Sidney Herbert Charrington was given temporary command of the 6th Northamptons as strategic positions were taken up prior to the attack.

At 7.00 pm on 13 July the attack on Trones Wood commenced and was met with fierce resistance. The advancing infantrymen faced intensive shelling as they moved into position, over open ground, towards the wood. Many men were also lost by accurate German sniper fire and strategically placed machine gun nests.

Fighting in the wood was now extremely hazardous. Days of bombardment and hand-to-hand fighting had brought down trees and branches resulting in almost impassable conditions on the ground. Sadly, added to this were the bodies of fallen soldiers, abandoned equipment, barbed wire, tangled undergrowth and all the debris of close combat warfare to be negotiated. Amazingly, there were a handful of open spaces littered with shell holes which presented additional hazards to

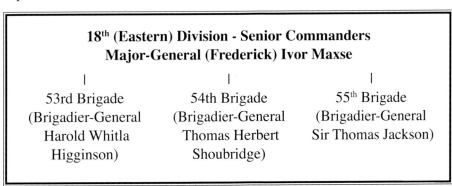

18th (Eastern) Division - Senior Commanders
Major-General (Frederick) Ivor Maxse

53rd Brigade	54th Brigade	55th Brigade
(Brigadier-General	(Brigadier-General	(Brigadier-General
Harold Whitla	Thomas Herbert	Sir Thomas Jackson)
Higginson)	Shoubridge)	

Men of the 18th Division carrying bombs forward in readiness for the attack on Trones Wood (By permission of the Imperial War Museum Q4052)

attacking troops in exposed positions.

The various attacking units faced heavy resistance with the 7th (Service) Battalion, The Queen's (Royal West Surrey Regiment) and the 7th (Service) Battalion, The Buffs (East Kent Regiment) being unable to make significant headway. However, isolated pockets of the 7th (Service) Battalion, Queen's Own (Royal West Kent Regiment) did reach the abandoned railway line which ran across the centre of Trones Wood.

By midnight the gallant attempt by units of the 55th Brigade of the 18th Division had failed to retake Trones Wood. Major-General Maxse was duly contacted by Lieutenant-General Walter Congreve VC the XIII Corps Commander to enquire as to his next move in a rapidly deteriorating situation. Maxse's response was that he would relieve his 55th Brigade by the 54th Brigade in a final desperate attempt to take the wood.

At 12.25 am Brigadier-General Shoubridge was ordered to attack with his 54th Brigade. Two battalions from the brigade were earmarked for the assault - the 12th Middlesex commanded by the redoubtable Lieutenant-Colonel Frank Maxwell VC and the 6th Northamptons under the command of Major Gerald Maitland Clark.

Brigadier-General Shoubridge then proceeded to make what was to prove to be a crucial decision. In view of serious difficulties in communication, due to telephone lines being destroyed by shell fire , he placed Lieutenant-Colonel Maxwell in overall command of the 6th Northamptons in addition to his own battalion, the 12th Middlesex.

At 2.30 am, Lieutenant-Colonel Maxwell went forward to the rendevous, at a sunken road approximately two thirds of a mile from Trones Wood, where troops of the two battalions were gathered in readiness for the attack. It had been his intention to lead the attack with his own battalion but in assessing the situation he discovered that the 6th Battalion of the Northamptons were fully assembled and ready to move, whereas only one company of his 12th Middlesex was in position.

Never one to ponder over what action to take Lieutenant-Colonel Maxwell quickly reversed the roles. This resulted in "The Steelbacks" becoming the attacking battalion supported by Maxwell's 12th Middlesex who took on the role of mopping up and flank defence.

Before reaching Trones Wood at 4.30am the Northamptons had been forced to cross one thousand yards of open ground. They quickly began to suffer casualties as they made their way through an intensive barrage of high explosive shells. They entered the wood at the south-west corner and before they had proceeded many yards they met with heavy rifle and machine gun fire. Tragedy struck when Major Clark who went forward to reconnoitre was shot and instantly killed. The command then passed to Major Sydney Charrington, the acting Commanding Officer.

Despite mounting casualties the overall commander, Lieutenant-Colonel Maxwell, gallantly gathered and led his surviving groups of 6th Northamptons and 12th Middlesex, with some isolated remnants of the 7th Royal West Kents (55th Brigade), in a line across the wood sweeping northwards and tackling anything which lay in their path.

When the railway line, running through the wood, was reached, a German machine gun, which hadn't been observed, opened fire. This serious obstacle was quickly overcome and put out of action.

The attacking force, firing as they made ground, advanced steadily ably led by Lieutenant-Colonel Maxwell. It was during the sweep towards the northern apex of the wood that the greatest danger was encountered – an enemy machine-gun situated at a critical point where the wood narrowed and covering an area of open ground. Spraying the ground ahead of them the German gunners were inflicting heavy casualties particularly amongst the advancing Northamptons.

By this time Sergeant William Boulter had taken command of his platoon following the loss of all of his officers. Assessing the situation ahead of him he quickly realized that he had to seize the initiative and, without a moment's thought for his

German Observation Post mounted in a tree in Trones Wood
(By permission of the Imperial War Museum Q862)

own safety, he charged the machine-gun post, in the face of withering fire, single handedly, with his bag of bombs, across an area of open ground pitted with shell craters.

During this remarkable act of gallantry, Sergeant Boulter was severely wounded. Whilst bending down to pick up a bomb he was shot through the left shoulder by a German sniper. Despite this he continued to zigzag his way towards the machine-gun displaying, as he progressed, the calibre and determination of an extraordinary soldier.

Painting by Edgar Holloway of Sergeant Boulter attacking the German machine-gun post

Using all his skills as a grenade thrower, sheer athleticism and raw, indefinable courage he bombed the enemy team from their position and silenced the deadly threat to his advancing comrades.

Sergeant Boulter finally fell exhausted within twenty yards of the machine-gun. After a few minutes, alone on the ground, he managed to get to his feet again. Typically, although bleeding profusely and in considerable pain, he walked back

unaided to the nearest dressing station, situated over two thousand yards behind the line, for urgent medical attention.

With the elimination of the remaining machine-gun, by Sergeant Boulter, the wood was finally cleared by 9.30 am and Major-General Maxse was able to report to his corps commander that Trones Wood was entirely in the hands of the 18th Division.

The 6th Battalion, The Northamptonshire Regiment suffered heavy casualties in the taking of the wood.

The 6th Battalion's losses in the capture of Trones Wood	
Killed	36
Wounded	204
Missing	35
Shell Shock	7
Total casualties	**282**

With the exception of Major Charrington and two young subalterns all the remaining officers had been killed or wounded.

The shattered remnants of Trones Wood 10 August 1916 (By permission of the Imperial War Museum Q861)

After the battle, Major-General Maxse described the soldiers of his 18th Division as "The boys to go fighting with." He was full of praise for the men of the 6th Northamptons, the 7th Royal West Kents (55th Brigade) and Lieutenant-Colonel Maxwell's 12th Middlesex Regiment.

Post being distributed at a base hospital to wounded men of the 6th Northamptons after their epic battle (Reproduced by permission of the Northampton Chronicle & Echo)

In his subsequent official report, after the completion of the taking of Trones Wood, Major-General Maxse wrote "No praise is too high for the gallantry and determination shown by the 6th Northamptons."

The German defenders had fought ferociously and courageously having received orders that they must hold the wood at all costs. In the men of the 6th Battalion, The Northamptonshire Regiment they had met their match. A compliment paid to them by one of the German prisoners recorded the admiration which he and his comrades felt: "We don't like you 'black patch' men as you never turn back."

The distinctive black patch, worn by the Northamptons, consisted of a small cloth black bar worn on the upper arm of the soldiers' tunics. The black patch was worn in memory of General James Wolfe who was killed at the Battle of Quebec in 1759. Both the 48th and 58th Regiments of Foot took part as units of General Wolfe's force which won a famous victory.

The situation, by the evening of 14 July, revealed that the Fourth Army had captured the villages of Bazentin-le-Petit, Bazentin-le-Grand also Longueval, with the exception of the northern part of the village, together with a number of strongly defended woods on the ridge.

Longueval proved to be a very difficult objective to secure due to stubborn and determined resistance by the German defenders.

The ruined village of Longueval after the battle (By permission of the Imperial War Museum Q1225)

5th Northern General Hospital, Leicester (Derek Seaton)

The entrance lodge which was located to the right of the gates to the 5th Northern General Hospital (Derek Seaton)

For Sergeant William Boulter his heroic part in the Battle of the Somme was over. After receiving further treatment at a casualty clearing station, the severity of his wound was considered to be so serious that on Sunday 16 July he was on his way back to England.

The hospital ship landed at Southampton on 17 July and he was admitted to hospital there the following day. On 19 July he was admitted to Litchfield Military Hospital where he received surgical treatment to his badly injured left shoulder.

On 7 September he was transferred to the 5th Northern General Hospital, Leicester which enabled him to be near to his family at Wigston Magna some three miles from the military hospital.

The 5th Northern General Hospital was formerly the Leicestershire and Rutland Lunatic Asylum built in 1836-7 (William Parsons). Today it is the Fielding Johnson building of the University of Leicester and is a Grade II listed building.

Whilst receiving treatment at the 5th Northern General Hospital Sergeant Boulter encountered a setback. When his wound had virtually healed, X-rays revealed a piece of decayed bone. Further surgery was required in order to reopen his shoulder and remove a fragment of bone.

During this time of surgical treatment and recovery, Sergeant Boulter was unaware that he had been recommended for the award of the Victoria Cross. He could only follow from afar the fortunes of his beloved 6th Battalion, the Northamptonshires, as they prepared for their next big battle at Thiepval in September 1916.

The Thiepval Ridge commanded a strategic position with an unobstructed view over the Albert area. For two long years the German Army had stubbornly held the ridge against repeated attacks by the British and French forces. On 26 September the 18th Division, with its 53rd and 54th Brigades as the attacking brigades, prepared to assault what the enemy described as "an impregnable position" the ruined village of Thiepval.

Three battalions of the 54th Brigade were selected for the assault: the 11th Royal Fusiliers, the 6th Northamptonshires and Lieutenant-Colonel Maxwell's 12th Middlesex Regiment with the 7th Bedfordshires in reserve. As they advanced over very difficult ground, ploughed up by shell fire, they encountered the full ferocity of a desperate enemy clinging to a heavily defended position on the ridge.

Whilst attempting to move the Battalion Headquarters forward, Lieutenant-Colonel Ripley and the Adjutant, Lieutenant W.H. Barkham were both seriously wounded by a shell which landed nearby. Once again Major Charrington assumed temporary command of the battalion. Lieutenant-Colonel Ripley was hit in the right arm by shrapnel which shattered the limb and caused severe damage to the bones in his arm.

By 6.00pm, after sustaining heavy casualties, the remains of the village of Thiepval, with the exception of one strongly defended corner to the north-west, had been taken by the elite fighting 54th Brigade commanded by Brigadier-General Thomas Shoubridge.

This latest success by the redoubtable 6th (Service) Battalion of the Northamptons was extremely costly, the casualties amounting to one third of the unit's strength.

The 6th Battalion's losses in the capture of Thiepval	
Killed	105
Wounded	235
Missing	23
Total casualties	**363**

Once again the 6th Battalion had fought magnificently against a formidable enemy. There was no greater admirer of their exploits than Sergeant William Boulter who avidly followed the actions of his battalion, from afar, with immense pride in the achievements of his comrades.

The ravages of war, on the Western Front, had reduced the once pretty village of Thiepval to a smouldering heap of rubble.

The huge number of wounded soldiers, including many of Sergeant Boulter's comrades and friends, were treated at the casualty clearing station at the rear of the battle area. The more seriously injured were taken to the larger 36th Casualty Clearing Station at Heilly, Mericourt-l'Abbe, by ambulance trains. Many British soldiers died from their wounds after the 1916 battles and were laid to rest in the nearby Heilly Station Cemetery.

Heilly Station Cemetery (Derek Seaton)

The ruins of Thiepval village from Thiepval Wood September 1916
(By permission of the Imperial War Museum Q1076)

German prisoners being marched to the rear after the Battle of Thiepval Ridge
(By permission of the Imperial War Museum Q1342)

The condition of Lieutenant-Colonel Ripley became a cause for concern, to all ranks, throughout the 6th Northamptons. His serious injury at the Battle of Thiepval necessitated the amputation of his right arm. Immediately, his wife Mrs Violet Jeanne Ripley arrived in France to be at her husband's bedside. Typically, he asked her to visit his wounded men. This kind gesture was greatly appreciated by every soldier who received an unexpected visit from the Colonel's wife.

During the second week of October 1916, Lieutenant-Colonel Ripley was taken back to England and admitted to a hospital in London. Tragically his condition rapidly deteriorated following the onset of tetanus, this led to a complete collapse and heart failure. On 16 October this gallant officer died and news of his death caused widespread pain and anguish throughout the entire 6th Battalion of his Regiment.

No one was more deeply distressed by the death of Lieutenant-Colonel Ripley than Sergeant Boulter. In a tribute to his late Commanding Officer he said of him: "No officer at the front was more loved. He was just like a father to us all thinking far more of our welfare and safety than is own. He was a thorough gentleman too."

Unknown to William Boulter one of the last acts of Lieutenant-Colonel Ripley was to recommend his gallant sergeant, from C Company, for the Victoria Cross.

Lieutenant-Colonel George Eustace Ripley outside of his tent (Reproduced by permission of the Northampton Chronicle & Echo)

The funeral of Lieutenant-Colonel Ripley took place at Cottingham, Northamptonshire on 19 October. His funeral took the form of the burial of a country gentlemen rather than a soldier. Six sergeants from the Northamptonshire Regiment formed a Guard of Honour and the Union Jack covered the coffin, otherwise the service was a simple one and devoid of military tributes. He was buried in the presence of The Right Honourable, The Earl Spencer, KG, PC, Lord-Lieutenant of Northamptonshire and leading representatives of the county.

This period was a low point for William Boulter. He was still recovering from his painful wound, he was away from his battalion and he had now lost his Commanding Officer whom he revered. However within a matter of days all was to change, despondency was to be replaced by widespread acclamation.

The Parish Church of St Mary Magdalene, Cottingham where Colonel Ripley's funeral service was held with his grave in the foreground. (Derek Seaton)

The Cottingham War Memorial with a panel bearing the name of Colonel Ripley and Private William Claypole also of the 6th (Service) Battalion, The Northamptonshire Regiment (Derek Seaton)

Sergeant Boulter was discharged from the 5th Northern General Hospital, Leicester on 21 October 1916 whereupon he was admitted to the British Red Cross Society Hospital at Green Hill, Belper, Derbyshire for a period of convalescence. Almost immediately he proceeded on sick leave to Kettering and then to his family's home at 9 Central Avenue, Wigston Magna, Leicestershire.

*9 Central Avenue, Wigston Magna, the Boulter family home in 1916
(Derek Seaton)*

*23766 Private Albert Boulter, 2nd Battalion, The Leicestershire Regiment
(Mrs Marion Partridge)*

By October 1916, Fred and Mary Boulter had three of their four sons serving in the British Army. Albert had enlisted into the Leicestershire Regiment and was serving, with the 2nd Battalion, in Mesopotamia. A skilled marksman he was deployed as a sniper. Harold, the youngest of the brothers, joined the Royal Army Medical Corps on 29 October 1915 having volunteered at the age of 19 years. He was stationed in England at the time.

The Boulter family had good reason to be proud of the contribution their boys were making for King and Country but suddenly, and unexpectedly their level of pride was to know no bounds. On Thursday 26 October, whilst having dinner with his family, a telegram arrived informing Sergeant Boulter that he had been awarded the Victoria Cross. The news caused great elation within the family, their neighbours and friends and throughout Wigston Magna.

*103331 Private Harold Boulter, Royal Army Medical Corps
(Mrs Eileen Vann)*

A prestigious list of fifteen recipients of the Victoria Cross had been published in the Fourth Supplement to *The London Gazette* (24 October 1916).

The official announcement in the press read as follows:

War Office, 26 October 1916

His Majesty The King has been graciously pleased to award the Victoria Cross to the undermentioned Officers, Non-commissioned Officers and Men:-

Major and Brevet Lieutenant-Colonel (temporary Lieutenant-Colonel)	**Coldstream Guards**
John Vaughan Campbell, DSO	
Bt. Major William La Touche Congreve, DSO, MC.	**Late Rifle Brigade**
Captain William Barnsley Allen, MC, MB.	**Royal Army Medical Corps**
Captain Noel Godfrey Chavasse, MC, MB.	**Royal Army Medical Corps**
Temporary Captain Archie Cecil Thomas White	**Yorkshire Regiment**
Lieutenant John Vincent Holland	**Leinster Regiment**
2nd Lieutenant Gabriel George Coury	**South Lancashire Regiment**
No 14603 Sergeant William Ewart Boulter	**Northamptonshire Regiment**
No 2815 Sergeant Albert Gill	**Late King's Royal Rifle Corps**
No 14951 Sergeant David James	**Liverpool Regiment**
No 13301 Lance-Sergeant Fred McNess	**Scots Guard**
No 73132 Private(Acting Corporal) Leo Clarke	**Canadian Infantry**
No 3/5027 Private Thomas Hughes	**Connaught Rangers**
No 11000 Private Thomas Alfred Jones	**Cheshire Regiment**
101465 Private John Chipman Kerr	**Canadian Infantry**

The individual citations were given in detail and, in the case of Sergeant Boulter, his citation read:

**No 14603 Sergeant William Ewart Boulter,
Northamptonshire Regiment**

For most conspicuous bravery. When one company and part of another were held up in the attack on a wood by a hostile machine-gun, which was causing heavy casualties, Sergeant Boulter, with utter contempt of danger and in spite of being severely wounded in the shoulder, advanced alone and over the open ground under heavy fire in front of the gun, and bombed the gun team from their position.

This very gallant act not only saved many casualties, but was of great military value, as it materially expedited the operation of clearing the enemy out of the wood, and thus covering the flank of the whole attacking force.

It would not have escaped Sergeant Boulter's notice that, included in the latest illustrous list, of those awarded the Victoria Cross, was the late Bt. Major William La Touche Congreve, DSO, MC, of The Rifle Brigade (Prince Consort's Own). He was the son of Lieutenant-General Walter Norris Congreve VC, the Corps Commander of XIII Corps of which the 18th (Eastern) Division was one of the divisions which had achieved considerable success in the Battle of the Somme.

Remarkably, the award of the Victoria Cross to Bt. Major Congreve, who was killed at Longueval on 20 July, emulated the gallantry of his father who, as a Captain in The Rifle Brigade, was awarded the Victoria Cross at the battle of Colenso on 15 December 1899 during the Boer War. Major William Congreve was also the first officer to be awarded the Victoria Cross, the Distinguished Service Order and the Military Cross.

The list also included Captain Noel Godfrey Chavasse, MC,MB, Royal Army Medical Corps, who later was awarded a Bar to his Victoria Cross on 2 August 1917 at Wieltje, Belgium. Captain

Sergeant Boulter in the garden of the family home at 9 Central Avenue, Wigston Magna with (left to right) his father Fred, younger sister Sarah and his mother Mary. Inset his brother Harold
(Jeremy Birkett)

Chavasse subsequently died of wounds received in action.

News of Sergeant Boulter's award quickly reached the local press and the family home was instantly besieged by reporters and photographers from the Leicester, Kettering and Northampton newspapers anxious to cover the story. Becoming the centre of media attention, and being acclaimed as a hero, did not rest easily with Sergeant Boulter. By nature, modest and unassuming he found it difficult to deal with the newly-acquired status as one who had displayed "most conspicuous bravery." Throughout an intensive series of interviews he maintained that he had: "Only done my bit as others had done." He was also quoted in the *Leicester Daily Mercury,* when referring to his part in the action at Trones wood: "It was the only thing to do and so I did it."

One sincere and penetrating description of William Boulter the man came from his friend and fellow senior NCO, Sergeant George Sismey who had been wounded on 31 March 1916. In a tribute to Sergeant Boulter, which appeared in the *Northampton Mercury* (27 October 1916) Sergeant Sismey said of him:

> *"He was a fine fellow, a thorough sportsman, a brave and daring soldier and one who was always bright and cheerful. He was a popular NCO, the sort to put heart into his men because he never lost heart himself. He was with us at Shorncliffe, Colchester and Codford St Mary and wherever he was he made friends for he had an attractive personality. He was fond of a joke and used to keep us alive when in training and he was just the same in the trenches. The men all liked him."*

Later in the war Sergeant Sismey was promoted to Warrant Officer (Class II) and was awarded the Distinguished Conduct Medal.

When visited by a reporter from *The Northampton Independent*, Sergeant Boulter warmly welcomed him into the family home commenting that: "The *Independent* has been so good to our boys at the front." The newspaper's readers had generously kept the men supplied with comforts. He briefly described the action at Trones Wood and his part in the attack upon the machine-gun post. Sergeant Boulter informed the reporter that he had been hit in the left shoulder by a sniper whilst picking up a bomb and that, in his view: "If I had been standing at the time, I don't think I'd be here." He went on to say that he was able to continue to advance alone and concluded the interview: "Well you know the rest."

He wasn't prepared to comment further upon his act of heroism but did add that just before he went forward to face the Germany machine-gun post, he had a narrow escape. A shell landed near to him and severely wounded one of his comrades. Sergeant Boulter said of the incident: "One of my chums Lance-Corporal Frederick Cordaroy of Northampton was hit by nineteen pieces of shrapnel but I escaped unhurt."

Photographs of William Boulter, with members of his family, were requested by the local newspapers, and the group photographs featured in the various publications in Leicestershire and Northamptonshire. Also in demand, to be included in the photographs, was Miss Florence Lusher who by this time was engaged to Billy.

Sergeant Boulter with a helmet worn by soldiers of the German 106th Infantry Regiment, 58th Division (Jeremy Birkett)

He brought home a number of other souvenirs including buttons from Bavarian uniforms, a buckle damaged by a bullet, from the belt of a Prussian soldier and rounds of various kinds of ammunition (*Leicester Daily Mercury* 27 October 1916).

Another response to the news of Sergeant Boulter's award was a batch of telegrams of congratulations. A number were from officers of the Northamptonshire Regiment including one which read:

Sergeant Boulter in a family group photographed at the Wigston Hosiery Society's factory in Paddock Street, Wigston Magna (left to right) Miss Florence Lusher, fiancée, his father Fred, brother Harold and his mother Mary (Jeremy Birkett)

> Very warmest congratulations and good wishes
>
> H.B. Simpson
> Captain
> 6th Northamptonshires

Individual pictures of the gallant soldier were also in demand and one striking photograph was taken of Sergeant Boulter, in the garden of the family home, displaying one of his souvenirs brought back from the Western Front.

He also received a telegram from the Drapery Department and other departments of the Kettering Industrial Co-operative Society Ltd. Nearer home a telegram came from Leicester which contained the message:

> Heartiest congratulations to our hero from the girls, Millinery Department
>
> Leicester Co-operative Society

One of Sergeant Boulter's most treasured messages of congratulations came from Mrs Violet Ripley, the widow of his late revered Commanding Officer. The message which was passed through a friend of Mrs Ripley, read:

> *"Will you give him my heartiest congratulations on his splendid achievement. Colonel Ripley, when home in September, told me one of his Sergeants had done splendidly and he hoped he would get a Victoria Cross. I know how the Colonel would have rejoiced had he lived to see the honour conferred, for it is a great thing for the dear old 6th to have a Victoria Cross to add to their list of distinctions."*

He was deeply touched by this thoughtful communication from Mrs Ripley.

The many photographs and telegrams were carefully preserved by Sergeant Boulter. He pasted them into a scrapbook. This book was a gift from his elder sister Mabel which she inscribed on the inside cover:

> *"To Will from Mabel*
> *11th November 1916"*

The scrapbook was to remain one of his treasured possessions.

As he struggled to regain his composure, Sergeant Boulter was almost overwhelmed with invitations to attend receptions, to be held in his honour, at Wigston Magna, Kettering and Northampton.

The first venue was William Boulter's adopted home town of Kettering where a Civic Reception was organised to take place on Saturday, 28 October. At 3.00pm he was met by Councillor Edward Chander Gravestock JP, the Chairman and members of the Kettering Urban District Council and representatives of the Kettering Industrial Co-operative Society Ltd.

Sergeant Boulter being welcomed by Councillor E.C. Gravestock JP and members of the Kettering Urban District Council (Reproduced by permission of the Northampton Chronicle & Echo)

A decorated motor car was provided for Sergeant Boulter, his fiancée Miss Lusher, his parents and Councillor Gravestock to take part in a procession drawn up to honour Kettering's first recipient of the Victoria Cross. The procession proceeded from Rockingham Road through the town to the Market Hill.

Sergeant Boulter and his party in the specially decorated motor car (Reproduced by permission of the Northampton Chronicle & Echo)

Preceded by the Band of the Kettering Rifles, the mounted Guard of Honour was provided by troops from the Remount Depot in Kettering. Sergeant

Boulter's car was followed by officers, NCOs and men of the Volunteer Training Corps, the Kettering Fire Brigade, St John Ambulance Brigade, the Boy Scouts, Girl Guides and the Church Lads' Brigade. Vast crowds lined the streets to give their "adopted son" an emotional and heartfelt welcome. Numerous flags were flying from the public buildings, and many private properties were decorated to mark the occasion.

A brief halt was made outside of Sergeant Boulter's workplace, the Drapery Department of the Kettering Industrial Co-operative Society Ltd in Newland Street. A Miss Weston made a presentation, on behalf of the staff, of a buttonhole for their deeply respected colleague and friend and an attractive bouquet for his fiancée.

Upon reaching the Market Hill he was received by Mr John Chaston, Assistant Town Clerk and a host of dignitaries including Officers of The Northamptonshire Regiment and the Mayor of Northampton, Councillor Joseph Pearse.

A temporary platform had been hastily erected in the Market Square, in front of the former Corn Exchange, where Sergeant Boulter was warmly welcomed by Councillor Gravestock who presided at the gathering.

The huge crowd of well-wishers and military escort gathered in the Market Square (Mrs Marion Partridge)

William Boulter received congratulations from the town of Kettering in the form of a resolution read out by the Assistant Town Clerk. Other tributes came from the Mayor of Northampton and, appropriately, from Captain Wallace Willows, a Company Commander in the 6th (Service) Battalion, The Northamptonshire Regiment. Captain Willows said that he too: "Had shared some of the privations to which Sergeant Boulter

had been subjected" and he was proud to be present to honour: "So good and brave a man."

In reply Sergeant Boulter said he hardly know how to express his thanks, he had only done his duty and felt that he did not deserve all the adulation. In his view every soldier in the Somme deserved praise as much as he did. He concluded by saying: "All the boys in the 6th Battalion would be pleased to know how well Kettering had treated him that day."

His father Fred also addressed the large gathering. He told the crowd that he was exceedingly proud of his son but: "No more proud of him now than when he went out to do his bit."

Fred Boulter addressing the crowd in Kettering Market Place; to his right is his youngest son, Private Harold Boulter, RAMC, Miss Florence Lusher and Sergeant Boulter (Jeremy Birkett)

Both Sergeant Boulter and his father received loud and prolonged cheers from the crowd before the reception was concluded with the singing of the National Anthem. Mr William Ballard, the Manager of the Kettering Industrial Co-operative Society Ltd, then entertained Sergeant Boulter and his family to tea at the Liberal Club.

The following day, Sunday 29 October, Billy Boulter attended the Old Adult School in Kettering, of which he was a member, where he received a warm welcome and congratulations from all the members many of whom were close friends.

He also received a letter of congratulations and good wishes from the Kettering Thursday Football Club of which he was a popular member and from whose ranks he, and six of his friends, had enlisted

Wigston VC holder visits his old school. Sergeant Boulter (in centre with stick), also in the group are Mr J.D. Broughton extreme left, Councillor J.W. Black JP, fifth from the left, father Fred Boulter, sixth from the left, brother Private Harold Boulter, seventh from right, his mother Mary sixth from right, sister Sarah fourth from right and Captain W.A. Brockington second from right. (Leicester Mercury)

in the 6th Battalion of "The Steelbacks" two years earlier.

A further tribute to Sergeant Boulter appeared in the local press from his former landlady, Mrs Elizabeth Shuffle who said of him: "He's a lovely boy, we liked him from the very first."

Then came a week of a hectic round of receptions and appearances which would test Sergeant Boulter's stamina to the full. He was, by this time, recovering well from the severe wound which had incapacitated him for the previous three months. Realizing that everyone wanted to congratulate him and wish him well, he accepted all the demands made of him with dignity, charm and pleasantness.

On Monday 30 October he was honoured by his old school in his own village of Wigston Magna. The invitation came from County Councillor John Wycliffe Black JP, Chairman of the Managers of the school, by then the Council School in Long Street, to be present at a reception at the school at 11.30 am.

To meet him, in addition to the excited pupils, were Councillor Black who chaired the proceedings, Captain William Allport Brockington, County Director of Education, Mr Edwin Arthur Preston his former Headmaster and the succeeding Headmaster Mr Edgar Boulter. Other guests were Lieutenant R. King, Durham Light Infantry, a former teacher at the school, Lieutenant C.M.B. Boulter, Machine Gun Corps, a son of the Headmaster, and Mr John Daykin Broughton, a local Hosiery Manufacturer.

Sergeant Boulter was accompanied by his parents, his brother Harold on leave from the 35th Company, Royal Army Medical Corps, Millbank, London and his younger sister Sarah May, aged 12 years.

A picture of Sergeant Boulter with members of his family and those gathered to welcome him appeared in the *Leicester Daily Post* dated 31 October 1916.

Other guests, at the reception, were the Headmistress at Bell Street Infants' School, Miss Mary Ann Jacklin and his uncle Alonzo Boulter, a School Attendance Officer (with the Leicestershire County Council) who had responsibility for the Wigston, Glen Parva and Oadby schools.

Alonzo Boulter (Mrs Marion Partridge)

William Boulter's uncle Alonzo was quite a fearsome looking official whose appearance served as a detriment to non-attendance at school by local pupils! Certainly he would not have been particularly busy on that special day as every child, at Long Street School, would have striven to be present to welcome back the school's illustrious former scholar Billy Boulter.

Speeches were made by Councillor Black, Mr J.D. Broughton and the Headmaster, all paying tribute to Sergeant Boulter's gallantry and to testify to the immense pride felt throughout the school, at the news that he had become Wigston Magna's first recipient of the Victoria Cross.

The Headmaster, Mr Edgar Boulter, in congratulating "the distinguished soldier" upon his award commented: "Some 300 old scholars were taking part in the war and nearly 20 of them had made the great sacrifice."

Responding, Sergeant Boulter said he hardly knew how to thank those who had spoken so kindly of him. Addressing the pupils he said he hoped that the boys and girls would have good luck and there would be no more wars for them to participate in.

In commemoration of the event the pupils were given a half-day holiday announced by Councillor Black as a: "Boulter half-holiday." Miss Jacklin was also to record in the Log Book of the Bell Street Infants' School:

---

3 November 1916. A half-holiday was allowed on Monday in honour of an old scholar, Sergeant W.E.Boulter who has won the Victoria Cross.

Miss Mary Ann Jacklin came from Litcham near Swaffham in Norfolk. She commenced as a Certified Assistant, at the school, on 29 October 1900 and was appointed Headmistress on 6 January 1902, a post she was to hold for twenty-five years.

The reception was concluded with the pupils giving three cheers for Sergeant Boulter and the singing of the National Anthem. A photograph of William Ewart Boulter VC was later placed in the school hall to remind future generations of his gallantry and award.

It was back to Kettering again on Thursday 2 November for the reluctant hero when he was honoured by his former employers, the Kettering Industrial Co-operative Society Ltd. He was the guest at a tea party followed by musical entertainment.

Mr William Ballard, the Society's Manager, spoke of the high appreciation of the employees and the management of Sergeant Boulter's bravery. A letter was also read out from Lord Channing of Wellingborough, the former Member of Parliament for Eastern Northamptonshire, who wrote to him: "I congratulate you with all my heart" and added "I do hope you will soon be free from all your trouble from your wound and completely regain your health."

He was then presented with a gold watch and chain. The watch was an English hunter made by Andrews Co-operative Watch Manufacturing Society, Coventry. Arrangements had been put in hand for the watch to be inscribed, on the inside, to read:

"Presented to Sergeant Boulter VC by the Kettering Industrial Co-operative Society in commemoration of his courageous act at Trones Wood, France, July 14, 1916"

The week ended with a most impressive reception at Northampton, on Saturday 4 November, where thousands of people gathered to honour Sergeant Boulter. Once again he was accompanied by his parents and his fiancée. Upon arriving in Northampton, shortly before 1.00pm, they were met by representatives of the Northampton Co-operative Wholesale Society who entertained him, and his guests, to lunch. Sergeant Boulter was presented with a marble timepiece, suitably inscribed, to mark the occasion.

At 2.30pm he was received at the Headquarters of The Northamptonshire Regiment, at Gibraltar Barracks on Barrack Road, by Colonel W.F. Fawcett who welcomed him and congratulated him on behalf of his Regiment.

Also there to greet him was the Mayor of Northampton, Councillor Joseph Pearse, the Mayoress and the Town Clerk, Mr Herbert Hankinson. A large procession was lined up to

Sergeant Boulter VC being received at the Regimental Depot by Colonel W.F. Fawcett, on the right is Major W.R. Woodham (Reproduced by permission of the Northampton Chronicle & Echo)

Sergeant Boulter VC chatting with the Mayoress of Northampton, Mrs J.E. Pearse, accompanied by his father and mother (Reproduced by permission of the Northampton Chronicle & Echo)

accompany Sergeant Boulter through the streets of the town, now thronged with people, as excitement grew.

The procession, which left Gibraltar Barracks at 3.15pm lined up as follows:

> The Band of the Volunteer Training Corps
>
> Troops from the Depot
>
> An open landau containing the Mayor with Sergeant Boulter VC, Colonel Fawcett and the Town Clerk
>
> Carriages containing Sergeant Boulter's parents, his fiancée and officers of his Regiment

The landau was drawn by ropes, pulled by men of the Northamptonshire Regiment, along the route from Barrack Road through the town and out on to the Wellingborough Road to its destination at Abington Park where a Civic Reception awaited the hero of the hour.

The procession passed Northampton's magnificent 19th century Guildhall where, during the previous two and half weeks, the Borough Council had been planning the day's itinerary and the form of presentation to be made to Sergeant Boulter.

This splendid neo-Gothic building was erected as the new Town Hall in St Giles' Square. The Eastern section was designed by Edward Godwin of Bristol and was opened in 1864. The Western

Sergeant Boulter VC with the Mayor, Colonel Fawcett and the Town Clerk leaving the Regimental Depot (Reproduced by permission of the Northampton Chronicle & Echo)

The Guildhall, St Giles' Square, Northampton (Derek Seaton)

The Bandstand (Derek Seaton)

extension was the work of Matthew Holding and A.W. Jeffery and was completed in 1892.

Along the route, decorated with flags and bunting, soldiers billeted in the town stood to attention and saluted as the landau passed. It was a deeply emotional experience for Sergeant Boulter particularly when he passed a number of severely wounded comrades who were lying in wheeled carriages. Their nurses gently raised them in order that they could get a good view of him. They cheered him loudly and he responded with a smile and saluted them several times, deeply conscious of their contribution and the suffering they were enduring.

The procession finally reached Abington Park where a Guard of Honour was assembled consisting of the Voluntary Aid Detachment, three companies of Girl Guides, a hundred and fifty Boy Scouts and cadets of the Church Lads' Brigade.

An area between the bandstand and the Abbey had been made into a reserved enclosure for ticket holders including the Mayoress- elect, Mrs John Woods.

Abington Abbey was built as a Manor House for John Bernard and his family in the 15th Century and was significantly enlarged in the 17th century. It became known later as Abington Abbey and is a Grade I listed building.

It was estimated that 20,000 people had assembled in Abington Park when the Major opened the proceedings. Councillor Pearse, on behalf of the town, made two presentations to Sergeant Boulter. The unique gifts consisted of an

Abington Abbey (Derek Seaton)

18 carat gold Waltham lever wristwatch engraved on the back with the Borough Arms and the wording:

"To Sergeant W.E. Boulter VC,
From the town of Northampton
November 4, 1916"

The Illuminated Address presented to Sergeant W.E. Boulter VC (Jeremy Birkett)

The second gift was a beautiful illuminated address, which had been framed and read as follows:

To Sergeant William Ewart Boulter VC
6th Battalion, Northamptonshire Regiment

"The County Borough of Northampton extends to you a hearty welcome and asks your acceptance of this address and a gold watch in token of our appreciation of your heroic conduct which has won for you the highest of all military honours, the Victoria Cross for most conspicuous bravery. We have read with pride in the official record of your achievement, how on July 14th, 1916, when one company of your battalion and part of another were held up in the attack on Trones Wood by a hostile machine-gun, which was causing heavy casualties, you, with utter disregard of danger, and in spite of being severely wounded in the shoulder, advanced alone over the open under heavy fire in front of the gun, and bombed the gun team from their position. Your very gallant act not only saved many casualties, but was of great military value, as it materially expedited the operation of clearing the enemy out of the wood, thus covering the flank of the whole attacking force and enabling the 6th Battalion of the Northamptonshire Regiment to capture and consolidate their position in the Germany stronghold which the enemy had proclaimed to be impregnable. Your valour has shed an additional lustre on the glorious Roll of Honour of our County Regiment, which has borne such a great and gallant part in the war. May you live long to enjoy the highest honour you have so worthily won.

Given under the Common Seal of the Corporation of Northampton this 4th day of November, 1916.

"J.E. PEARSE,
Mayor
H. HANKINSON,
Town Clerk"

In his heartfelt and sincere speech of thanks, for all the honours which Northampton had bestowed upon him that day, Sergeant Boulter asked the great assembly to remember the boys at the front and see to it that they were not lacking in comforts. He expressed the hope that all his comrades would receive parcels, from the people of Northampton, in time for Christmas.

At the close of the ceremony, the Mayor called for three cheers for Sergeant Boulter. This was followed by the playing of the Regimental March of The Northamptonshire Regiment and the National Anthem.

Later William Boulter and his guests were entertained to tea by the Borough Council in the Grand Hotel. Thus ended a day he would never forget.

On Tuesday, 7 November, Sergeant Boulter was again honoured during a busy week in London. He was the guest of honour at the annual sale day of the Co-operative Wholesale Society. After speeches of congratulations by the officers of the Society, he was presented with a "handsome smoker's cabinet." This was a most appropriate gift as William Boulter had always derived great enjoyment from smoking cigarettes.

During the afternoon he visited the House of Commons followed by a visit to the House of Lords where he listened to a debate. He was then entertained to tea by Lord Channing of Wellingborough and Lord Charnwood.

The final public reception for Sergeant Boulter, took place, appropriately, in his own village of Wigston Magna, Leicestershire, on Saturday 9 December. He was invited, together with his parents, his younger sister Sarah May and his fiancée Miss Lusher to receive the acclamations of those who lived in the place where his father's family had their roots.

Initially, they were invited to the Regimental Depot of The Leicestershire Regiment at their nearby Glen Parva Barracks where the day's proceedings commenced.

A procession headed by a military band and a

Glen Parva Barracks, South Wigston (Duncan Lucas)

detachment of soldiers left the barracks. Sergeant Boulter and his family travelled in the first horse-drawn carriage with other carriages and motor cars conveying local dignitaries and officials. The Great Wigston United and the Wigston Temperance Prize massed bands, the Wigston and Glen Parva V.T.O and a detachment of Boy Scouts also formed part of the procession.

People lined the route to give a warm welcome to their local hero as the procession made its way through Wigston Magna passing by Central Avenue where the Boulter family lived. They finally arrived at The Fountain (also known as The Bank), in the centre of the village, at the top of Bull Head Street where Billy was born.

A temporary platform consisted of a cart belonging to Councillor Eli Bailey, a carter and farmer and a member of the Wigston Urban District Council. The event was described in the *Illustrated Leicester Chronicle* accompanied by a splendid photograph of the occasion.

William Boulter received a tremendous ovation from a huge crowd. The Chairman, Councillor A. E. Hill JP welcomed him and said: "Not only had

The Fountain, Wigston Magna (Duncan Lucas)

he done his duty but he had brought honour to himself and his native village." Councillor Black reminded the onlookers: "In Leicestershire they only had two VCs during the present war, one given to a Wigston man and the other to a soldier who had been brought up two and a half miles from Wigston." He was referring to the late Private William Henry Buckingham VC, the former Countesthorpe Cottage Homes boy, of the 2nd Battalion, The Leicestershire Regiment, who had been awarded the Victoria Cross at the Battle of Neuve Chapelle in March 1915.

Sergeant William Boulter VC with members of his family and local dignitaries (Left to right) Sgt Boulter VC, his mother Mary Ann, his fiancée Miss Florence Lusher, his father Fred, Councillor Albert Edward Hill JP (Chairman of the Wigston U.D.C.), Councillor John Wycliffe Black JP (Vice-Chairman) and sitting at the rear (partly hidden) Councillor Harry Thorpe Hincks (Leicester Mercury)

Councillor Hill presented Sergeant Boulter with a bronze shield, in repoussé work, mounted on oak, bearing the inscription:

> *"Presented to Sergeant William Ewart Boulter VC, Northamptonshire Regiment by the residents of Wigston Magna - his native place - as a mark of appreciation for his conspicuous bravery in the field and to commemorate the honour which has been conferred upon him by His Majesty The King December 1916"*

Private William Henry Buckingham VC, walking with some of the boys on the drive at the Cottage Homes (The Record Office for Leicestershire, Leicester & Rutland)

It was intimated that another gift to the value of £100 would follow later.

In thanking everyone concerned, Sergeant Boulter said he was one of the first to admit that many VCs had been won on the battlefield but the deeds had not been recognised. He only hoped that a better method of settling disputes, other than by war, could be found in the future.

On 1 January 1917, Major-General Ivor Maxse was promoted to Lieutenant-General and received a Knighthood. He was given command of XVIII Corps, a new corps for which he assumed responsibility for its formation. As a career soldier Sir Ivor was obviously delighted with his promotion, for which he had been earmarked, nevertheless it was with great sadness that he bade his goodbyes to the 18th (Eastern) Division. He said of his beloved 18th he hated leaving the division: "Because it has such a series of unbroken successes in battle."

In a direct reference to Sergeant Boulter, his former divisional commander once said of him: "It was always difficult to persuade him to describe his exploit." Lieutenant-General Sir Ivor Maxse went on to comment: "As a rule, all he would say was that he had with him that morning a revolver that kept going off, and so he killed Germans."

By early 1917 Sergeant Boulter's wound to his left shoulder had healed to the point where he was able to return to active service. During his period of recovery he had given a great deal of thought to his future as a soldier and decided to apply for admission to an Officer Cadet Unit with a view to gaining a temporary commission. He duly completed the application forms on 18 January 1917, whilst stationed at the Ampthill Command Depot in Bedfordshire, and expressed a wish to be commissioned into The Northamptonshire Regiment.

He was certified as being fit again for military service, his weight was now 11 stone 11 lbs in contrast to the 9 stone 5 lbs recorded when he enlisted in September 1914. He was certified to be of 'good moral character' by Councillor A.E. Hill JP, who had known him for the previous ten years, and lived a short distance from the Boulter family home. Councillor Hill, and his family, lived at The Grange which was situated in private grounds, off the left-hand side of Leicester Road, on the approach into Wigston Magna from the city.

The Grange was built in c.1825 by John

The Grange, Wigston Magna, the home of Councillor Albert Edward Hill JP (Derek Seaton)

Burgess a yeoman farmer. His son Thomas was the owner by 1841; he was a Quaker, a wool stapler and a highly respected philanthropist. The building is now occupied by the Institution of Occupational Safety and Health.

Evidence that the candidate had attained a standard of education, suitable for commissioned rank, was given under the signature of Mr Edgar Boulter, the Headmaster of Wigston Magna Council School.

The certificate of recommendation, for admission to an Officer Cadet Unit, was signed by the Colonel commanding Ampthill Command Depot on 7 February. Sergeant Boulter's application was duly accepted and he was posted to No 13 Officer Cadet Battalion, at Newmarket, on 9 March.

Interestingly, the final entry on Sergeant Boulter's Regimental Conduct Sheet, before embarking upon Officer Cadet training, was the extract from *The London Gazette* (24 October 1916) headed:

> No 14603 Sergeant William Ewart Boulter, Northamptonshire Regiment awarded the Victoria Cross for gallantry in the Field

The citation was detailed fully and how it differed from the earlier entries of misdemeanours committed and punishments recorded on his Company Conduct Sheet. It could be said that the slate had been wiped clean!

During his time as an Officer Cadet he experienced the greatest honour that can befall any soldier serving in the British Army. On 12 March 1917 he received the following memorandum from the War Office:

Memorandum

From	**To**
A.G.4.d.	No 14603 Sergeant W.E. Boulter VC,
War Office,	6th Battalion, Northamptonshire Regiment,
London, S.W.	9 Central Avenue,
12 March 1917	Wigston, Leicester

You are required to attend at Buckingham Palace on Saturday next the 17th March 1916 to receive the Victoria Cross from His Majesty the King.

You should report yourself to the Regimental Sergeant Major 3/ Scots Guards, Wellington Barracks, London before 10.00pm on Friday 16th March 1917

Obtain from local Military authorities a Railway Warrant to cover your return journey. Please acknowledge receipt of these orders.

(signed) B. Leach
Colonel
A.A.G.
For Brigadier General,
Director of
Personal Services

On 15 March, Sergeant Boulter was issued with what can only be described as a most unusual leave pass, the wording of which was unique to that select band of servicemen being granted leave to receive the Victoria Cross from their Sovereign.

The essential details from his leave pass read as follows:

Regiment: No 13 Officer Cadet Battalion

14603 Sergeant W.E. Boulter VC
has permission to be absent from his quarters from
2.00pm 16.3.1917 to 11.55pm 18.3.1917
for the purpose of proceeding to London (Buckingham Palace) to receive the Victoria Cross from His Majesty The King

---

For William Boulter his great moment had arrived. On St Patrick's Day, Saturday 17 March he stood before His Majesty King George V who decorated him with the Victoria Cross. He was the sole recipient of the Victoria Cross at that particular investiture. It would not have escaped His Majesty's notice that Sergeant Boulter was, by this time, an Officer Cadet striving to obtain the King's commission.

By coincidence he was not the only soldier from Leicestershire to be honoured that day. His Majesty also invested Lieutenant-Colonel Robert Edmund Martin with the Insignia of Companion of The Most Distinguished Order of St. Michael and St George. Lieutenant-Colonel Martin had commanded the 1/4th Battalion, The Leicestershire Regiment, as part of the 46th (North Midland) Division, in the assault on the Hohenzollern Redoubt on 13 October 1915.

After a furious battle the Redoubt was captured but the Battalion's casualties were horrendous. Lieutenant-Colonel Martin was severely wounded

Sergeant Boulter VC outside Buckingham Palace after receiving his Victoria Cross from The King, he is wearing the white band of an Officer Cadet on his service cap

and, after 24 hours of action, the 1/4th Leicesters had lost 20 officers and 453 NCOs and men killed, wounded or missing.

Lieutenant-Colonel Robert Edmund Martin (Colonel Robert Martin)

By 1917 many of William Boulter's friends, from Wigston Magna, were serving in The Leicestershire Regiment and his brother Albert was with the 2nd Battalion of the Regiment in Mesopotamia. Undoubtedly these two gallant soldiers, Sergeant William Ewart Boulter VC and Lieutenant-Colonel Robert Edmund Martin CMG would have appreciated the opportunity to enjoy each other's company, for a short time, in the magnificent splendour of Buckingham Palace.

Upon emerging from the Palace, Sergeant Boulter was surrounded by enthusiastic well-wishers all wanting to congratulate him and to shake his hand.

After the unforgettable experience of receiving his Victoria Cross, William Boulter returned to Newmarket to complete his training. He coped admirably with the strenuous academic and physical demands of the Officer Cadet Training Course and was successful in his endeavours. *The London Gazette,* dated 24 July 1917, detailed a list of cadets appointed to the rank of 2nd Lieutenant. The list was headed:

> The undermentioned cadets to be
> Temporary 2nd Lieutenants
> 27 June 1917

Included amongst a large number of cadets shown by the regiments to which they had been posted appeared:

Northamptonshire Regiment - William Ewart Boulter VC

Navy on 8 August 1917 and did his initial training on HMS Victory. At that time Admiral Horatio Nelson's famous flagship was afloat off Gosport and was the flagship of Admiral The Honourable Sir Stanley Colville, Commander-in-Chief, Portsmouth.

2nd Lieutenant W.E. Boulter VC photographed in Leicester shortly after receiving his commission
(Mrs Marion Partridge)

P/J75666 Ordinary Seaman George Boulter
(Mrs Marion Partridge)

Meanwhile George, the eldest of the Boulter brothers had been conscripted into the Royal Navy. He had been employed in a key position at the Wigston Hosiery Society's factory where his father was the manager. George was in charge of the making-up of the garments during a period of intense activity with Government contracts to be fulfilled and huge demands being made upon the workforce.

Conscription was introduced as a result of the Military Service Act 1916 and, eventually George had to leave his post, important though it was in terms of the war effort, in order to follow his brothers into the forces. George joined the Royal

George later served as an Able Seaman, with the Home Fleet, on a number of auxiliary repair and depot ships at various shore establishments and at Scapa Flow.

Following the gaining of his commission, 2nd Lieutenant William Boulter was posted to the 7th (Service) Battalion of the Northamptonshire Regiment. He returned to France to join his new battalion in August 1917.

The 7th Battalion was predominately a battalion of sportsmen. It was formed in September 1914 and contained, within its ranks, hundreds of young sportsmen from Northamptonshire. Teams of 'pals' who played association football, rugby football, cricket and other sports joined *en masse* to answer the call to arms. A leading light in the formation of the 7th Battalion was Edgar Roberts Mobbs, the gifted England and Northampton Rugby Union player. Within forty-eight hours of a rallying recruitment call by Mobbs, 400 men assembled in Northampton to support him and from which a company of 250 was formed. The 7th Battalion left for France on 31 August 1915 and had its baptism of fire at the Battle of Loos, in the autumn of that year, as one of the units of the 24th Division.

Edgar Mobbs, who enlisted as a private soldier, went on to obtain a commission and rapidly gained promotion to reach the rank of Lieutenant-Colonel and to assume command of the 7th Battalion in February 1916. He was wounded on three occasions and was awarded the Distinguished Service Order on 1 January 1917.

The Third Battle of Ypres (Passchendaele) commenced on 31 July 1917. It was a dark day in the history of the 7th Northamptonshires as their inspirational Commanding Officer, Lieutenant-

Colonel Mobbs was killed on the opening day of the battle. In addition 3 other officers were killed and 8 wounded plus 246 casualties, within the ranks, in the successful attack, by the 24th Division, on Shrewsbury Forest, near to Zillebeke, in the Ypres Salient (Shrewsbury Forest was a wood so named after The King's Shropshire Light Infantry).

The following day (1 August), the severely depleted companies of the 7th Northamptonshires were withdrawn from the Front Line. They were relieved by the 1st Battalion, Prince of Wales's (North Staffordshire Regiment) and the 13th (Service) Battalion, Duke of Cambridge's Own (Middlesex Regiment).

The immediate task was to rebuild the battalion under the direction of the newly promoted Commanding Officer, Lieutenant-Colonel David Watson Powell. The new battalion commander, who had been gazetted into The Northamptonshire Regiment in 1900, had only arrived four weeks earlier when he was posted to the 7th Battalion as Second-in-Command.

The 7th (Service) Battalion, The Northamptonshire Regiment in camp near Dickebusch, Belgium, on 9 August 1917, resting after their attack on Shrewsbury Forest (By permission of the Imperial War Museum Q5847)

Men of the 7th Battalion drawing rations from the Quartermaster's Stores in camp at Dickebusch 9 August 1917 (By permission of The Imperial War Museum 5849)

The battalion's depleted ranks were reinforced by officers and men from the 2nd Battalion, Prince of Wales's Leinster Regiment (Royal Canadians), their comrades in the costly attack on Shrewsbury Forest where they too had suffered heavy losses. A composite battalion was formed from the two units.

Following a period of much needed rest and recuperation the 7th (Service) Battalion, The Northamptons was back in the line on 11 August. Two short periods in the Front Line followed.

The War Diary of the 7th Battalion, dated 30 August, recorded:

> The following officers joined today:
>
> 2nd/Lt W.E. Boulter VC, 2nd/Lt. L. Bostock and 2nd/Lt M.S. Gotch

By this time the 7th Battalion had been moved to "J" camp near to Dickebusch Brewery – a desirable location for British Tommies! It was affectionately known as Brewery Camp "J".

Following a further short spell in the line in the Ypres-Menin Road sector the battalion, along with other units of the 24th Division, prepared to move to the Somme area. After a brief period at Ypres it was back to the Somme battlefield for 2nd Lieutenant William Ewart Boulter.

The battalion was gradually moved, from 14 September onwards, in stages, by periods of marching and by motor buses to billets near to Steenwerck. Six days later they marched to Bailleul where they entrained for Bapaume. On 26 September they were back in action taking over trenches from the 21st (Service) Battalion, The Northumberland Fusiliers in the Hargicourt sector at St Quentin.

The entire area was a scene of utter devastation, practically all roads, bridges and woods had been destroyed. The trenches were waterlogged and surrounded by deep mud which made conditions for the troops almost unbearable. Only short periods of four days duration could, effectively, be spent in such appalling conditions. Whenever the men of the 7th Northamptons were out of the line, time was utilised on "rifle and feet inspections" as the winter began to close in across the battlefield.

The terrible conditions in the forward trenches caused havoc amongst the exhausted infantrymen. An early victim was Second-Lieutenant Boulter who contracted trench fever and acute bronchitis which necessitated him being withdrawn from his battalion on 16 October for medical treatment. By December he was convalescing in the south of France.

"All in step, with one pipe and four cigarettes!" 2nd Lieutenant William Boulter VC (second from left) with fellow officers, on convalescence, strolling along the promenade at Nice on 8 December 1917 (Jeremy Birkett)

Following this latest setback, 2nd Lieutenant Boulter was unable to regain a level of fitness which would allow him to return to active service. His wound, at Trones Wood in 1916 and his illnesses in 1917 had taken their toll.

Once again it became necessary for him to return to England for hospitalisation. On 26 February 1918, he embarked from Calais for Dover and the following day he was admitted to the 2nd Western General Hospital in Manchester. At that time twenty-six public buildings were being utilised by the 2nd Western General Hospital, in and around Manchester for the treatment of soldiers suffering from wounds and illnesses. The various units included many adapted school premises.

During the period 3 April to 13 May William Boulter was cared for in the 170 bedded Hospital for Officers situated in the High Street in Manchester.

On 2 October he was invalided to the Imperial Hospital, St Annes-on-Sea, Lancashire still suffering from the effects of trench fever. Whilst there he applied for employment under a Ministry of Labour Scheme for Officers University and Technical Classes (Professional and Business Register).

The long-awaited end to the Great War came on 11 November 1918. On that day 2nd Lieutenant Boulter appeared before his last Medical Board at the King's Lancashire Military Convalescent Hospital, Squires Gate, Blackpool and was again classified as unfit for general service.

He was successful in his application to the Ministry of Labour and assumed duty, under the scheme, at the Ministry's No 3 District, College of Technology, Sackville Street, Manchester on 28 November until he regained his fitness.

William Boulter's final accomplishment as a soldier came on 27 December 1918 when he was promoted to the rank of Lieutenant. He was finally released from the Army on 25 April 1919 whereupon he was required: "To relinquish your commission, upon completion of service, and to retain the rank of Lieutenant." Following discharge he remained employed by the Ministry of Labour, in the Army List, until August 1919.

After a distinguished period of military service, which had lasted for four years and seven months, Lieutenant Boulter VC was once again a civilian actively seeking employment in a world which had changed almost beyond comprehension.

Chapter Five - Life After The Western Front

By the end of 1919 the Boulter family was once again united in that, amazingly, all of Fred and Mary's four sons had survived and had returned home from the various theatres of war across the world. George, the eldest, was demobilised from the Royal Navy on 7 July 1919. Albert, who was wounded whilst serving in Mesopotamia had moved with the 2nd Battalion, The Leicestershire Regiment to India from where he eventually returned home.

George returned to work for the Wigston Hosiery Society where he became a driver, in addition to which he undertook the duties of chauffeur as and when required. This involved him in driving the President, Chairman and, on occasions, his father Fred as the Factory Manager.

Albert Boulter was assisted by his father who set him up in business in the hosiery trade. Later he worked for Nathaniel Corah and Sons Ltd, St Margaret's Works, Canning Street, Leicester. The huge factory covered an area of four acres and was opened in 1866. In less than twenty years this highly successful firm was employing 1,000 people.

Harold, the youngest of the brothers, served in Mesopotamia from 25 December 1916 to 31 December 1918 before leaving for Russia, with his unit, on 1 January 1919. Although the war had ended on 11 November 1918, the British Government dispatched an Expeditionary Force to northern Russia where the Allies had considerable quantities of supplies stockpiled. Whist attempting to safeguard the supplies, the British troops were drawn into action alongside the White Russian Army (formerly the forces of the late Tsar Nicholas II) against the Bolsheviks. Subsequently, Britain mounted the North Russia Relief Force, in June 1919, to effect the withdrawal of its forces. The involvement of the Boulter's youngest son in this further short-lived campaign caused additional anxiety to his family after the war was officially over.

Harold was eventually demobilised on 19 November 1919 having served for four years and fourteen days. Upon discharge he received a disability pension of eight shillings per week in respect of malaria fever contracted during his service. His degree of disablement was assessed at 20% and his case was noted "to be reviewed after fifty-two weeks". Eventually he overcame his illness.

After the war Harold worked in various grocery shops in Leicester before returning to work for the Wigston Co-operative Stores Ltd (later to become the Wigston Co-operative Society Ltd).

The departmental store of the Wigston Co-operative Stores Ltd in Long Street and Central Avenue, Wigston Magna (Duncan Lucas)

Harold Boulter went on to become the Branch Manager at the nearby Wigston Fields store.

By 1920, William Boulter had taken up residence in Northampton having joined the staff of the Northampton Chamber of Commerce journal and allied publications whose offices were located at Barclays Bank Chambers, St Giles' Square, in the centre of the town.

Lieutenant Boulter's links with his former comrades, particularly those who had served in the 6th (Service) Battalion of the Northamptonshires, remained important to him and would continue to do so throughout the remainder of his life. The 18th (Eastern) Division, in which the 6th Battalion had played such a glorious part, was to be remembered for all time on the Western Front in the form of two monuments which were erected at Trones Wood and at Thiepval. The monuments which were splendid obelisks were unveiled, appropriately, by Lieutenant-General Sir Ivor Maxse.

The 18th Division, which stood down on 19 March 1919, had the proud distinction of having gained eleven Victoria Crosses during its time on the Western Front. William Boulter was the first name which appeared on this illustrious list which

Monument to the 18th (Eastern) Division, Trones Wood, France (Derek Seaton)

was a testimony to a remarkable division of Kitchener's Second New Army.

A great military occasion took place in London, on Saturday, 26 June 1920, when King George V and Queen Mary invited all the holders of the Victoria Cross to a Garden Party, given in their honour, at Buckingham Palace. The King was personally involved in the planning of the event and it was his express wish that the people of London, and visitors, should have the opportunity to pay their tributes to "the bravest of the brave". (*The Times* 28 June 1920).

Invitation Card to the Garden Party - Lieutenant W.E. Boulter, VC (Jeremy Birkett)

The holders and their invited guests were entertained to luncheon, at Wellington Barracks, by the Officers of the Brigade of Guards.

Wellington Barracks and Parade Ground, Birdcage Walk, London (Derek Seaton)

Whilst at the Guards' Barracks, no doubt Lieutenant Boulter would have reflected upon the fact that his old divisional commander, the redoubtable Major-General Ivor Maxse once had his headquarters at Wellington Barracks. This was back in 1907 when he was appointed Regimental Lieutenant-Colonel, Coldstream Guards and worked in one of the small classical style buildings on the edge of the parade ground.

After what Lieutenant Boulter described as a "sumptuous lunch" the honoured guests mingled

Major-General Maxse's office at Wellington Barracks
(Derek Seaton)

in the courtyard prior to the commencement of the parade and march to Buckingham Palace.

These included Captain Samuel Meekosha who was awarded the Victoria Cross on 19 November 1915. At the time he was a corporal serving in the 1/6th Battalion, The West Yorkshire Regiment (Territorial Force). The citation *(The London Gazette* 22 January 1916) read:

No 1147 Corporal Samuel Meekosha,
1/6th Battalion The West Yorkshire Regiment
(Territorial Force)

For most conspicuous bravery near the Yser, France on 19 November 1915. He was with a platoon of about 20 non-commissioned officers and men who were holding an isolated trench.

During a very heavy bombardment by the enemy, six of the platoon were killed and seven were wounded, while all the remainder were more or less buried. When the senior non-commissioned officers had been either killed or wounded, Corporal Meekosha at once took command, sent a runner for assistance, and in spite of no less than ten more big shells falling within twenty yards of him, continued to dig out the wounded and buried men in full view of the enemy, and at close range from the German trenches. By his promptness and magnificent courage and determination he saved at least four lives.

Coincidently, both 2nd Lieutenant W.E. Boulter VC and 2nd Lieutenant S Meekosha VC were promoted to the rank of Lieutenant on the same date – 27 December 1918.

The 310 holders of the Victoria Cross, present on the day, were marshalled by services and

Lieutenant William Ewart Boulter VC, The Northamptonshire Regiment (right) chatting to Captain Samuel Meekosha VC, Corps of Military Accountants (created in 1919) prior to the march

regiments, in readiness for the march to Buckingham Palace. The unique parade marched out of Wellington Barracks led by the band of the Welsh Guards to be greeted by thousands of people who lined the route from Birdcage Walk via Horse Guards Parade and along The Mall to Buckingham Palace.

Buckingham Palace (Derek Seaton)

Upon reaching the Palace Gardens, the VC holders were re-formed in order of seniority of award and each recipient was received individually by The King wearing the service dress uniform of a Field Marshall. He was accompanied by Queen Mary and other members of the Royal Family.

Lieutenant Boulter said of the occasion, in an interview with *The Northampton Independent*, that His Majesty shook hands with him and with a pleasant smile said: "I am pleased to see you again" He went on to inform the reporter that nothing impressed him more than the spirit of comradeship at the gathering, he added: "Distinguished generals with their breasts ablaze with ribbons fraternising with privates".

Meanwhile, Billy's father, Fred, as the Factory Manager, shared in the celebrations to commemorate the "Coming of Age" of the Wigston Hosiery Society. During the first half of 1920 a period of twenty-one years of operating was completed. Fred Boulter had been a member of the Society since its onset and had held the position of manager for 11 years (1909-1920). Appropriate celebrations were enjoyed by the workers, shareholders and management to mark the occasion.

A return to his native county in 1921 saw William Boulter setting up in business, in Leicester, manufacturing ladies' stockings. For reasons unknown the romance between Miss Florence Lusher and Billy had not survived and, by this time, she no longer featured in his life.

In 1922 he acquired a business partner. He was joined by Leslie William Hurren and they established a small firm, Boulter and Hurren Ltd, knitted goods manufacturers, with premises at 10 & 12 Market Street, Leicester. The business premises were shared with Simon Sirkin & Co, furriers (Nos 10 & 12) and Gerald Robert Johnson, yarn agent (No 10).

Leslie Hurren had also served in the First World War, he was a private soldier in both the Royal Army Medical Corps and the Royal Engineers.

10 & 12 Market Street, Leicester (Derek Seaton)

The Committee of the Wigston Hosiery Society 1920 Fred Boulter (manager) is seated second from the right (Midlands Co-operative Society Ltd)

The Northamptonshire Regiment was blessed with one of the most magnificent Garrison Churches which any regiment could wish for. The Regimental Depot was located in the Parish of the Holy Sepulchre, Northampton which consequently became the spiritual home of the Northamptonshires. An original round church, the building was commenced in 1099 following the First Crusade. The church was extended, at different times, between the 12th and 14th centuries followed by a complete restoration, during the mid-Victorian period, by George Gilbert Scott which was completed in 1864. Of the nine round churches built in England, during the Middle Ages, the Church of the Holy Sepulchre is the largest and best preserved of the four remaining round churches.

The Church of the Holy Sepulchre Northampton (By kind permission of Holy Sepulchre Church)

After the First World War, additional regimental memorials were added to those already located within the Church of the Holy Sepulchre. A beautiful stained glass window in memory of Lieutenant-Colonel George Eustace Ripley, the Commanding Officer of the 6th Battalion, The Northamptonshire Regiment was unveiled on the Outer North Aisle.

The Regimental Window in memory of Lieutenant-Colonel George Eustace Ripley (By kind permission of Holy Sepulchre Church) (Derek Seaton)

In addition a window in the Chapel of St George, which is the Regimental Chapel, is dedicated to the 6th (Service) Battalion and depicts the Battle Honours gained on the Western Front. The Colours of the Battalion were laid up in the Chancel, along with those of the 5th and 7th (Service) Battalions.

By 1922 the various Campaign Medals for the First World War were being issued. Lieutenant Boulter received three medals to add to his Victoria Cross – the 1914-15 star, the British War Medal and the Victory Medal.

William Boulter captured the headlines on the front page of the *Leicester Mercury* on Wednesday 9 September 1925 in a way he would not have wished. The headline read:

LEICESTER VC THREATENED

At a hearing at Leicester Police Court, that afternoon, William Ewart Boulter VC, aged 32, and Leslie William Hurren, aged 28, were summoned for giving false information to a police constable regarding a French business employee Mademoiselle Lea Irma Jarquart.

The prosecution alleged that the partners had engaged Mlle Jarcourt to introduce them to markets and outlets in France. They had not, however, obtained an Home Office permit to employ her as required by the Aliens Act. An agent, in France, had written letters to the partners Boulter and Hurren attempting to blackmail them by threatening to inform the Leicester police unless Lea Jarquart returned to France. This he eventually did which led to all three being charged and to which they pleaded guilty.

The firm of Boulter and Hurren Ltd had certainly expanded its production as a result of Mademoiselle Jarquart joining the firm. The increased output had enabled them to take on five male employees whereas previously they employed no one. Their range of products had also increased to include the manufacture of gowns and sportswear.

Following guilty verdicts, the Magistrates imposed fines of £15 on each of the defendants and two guineas costs. The Mayor, Councillor Herbert Simpson, although obliged to enforce the law said that he saw no reason why Mademoiselle Jarquart should be deported. He applauded the refusal of William Boulter and Leslie Hurren to accede to the blackmail requests.

1927 proved to be quite a momentous year for William Boulter. Firstly, he moved onto the London scene to become the Manager of a large firm of hosiery manufacturers Messrs T.H. Downing & Co Ltd, 3A Wood Street, London E.C.2. His knowledge of the hosiery trade and his increasing managerial skills replicated his father's considerable achievements.

Billy Boulter's happiness became complete, in the spring of 1927, when he married a lady who was born less than two miles away from his own place of birth in Wigston Magna, Leicestershire. His bride was Miss Alice Irene Toone, the daughter of Benjamin Toone junior a boot and shoe manufacturer and his wife Sarah Hannah Toone. Irene was born, at the family home, Stratford Villa, Clifford Street, South Wigston on 31 October 1897.

Clifford Street, South Wigston, Leicestershire (Derek Seaton)

Benjamin Toone was a successful local businessman in South Wigston having followed his father Benjamin Toone senior into the manufacturing of footwear.

Prior to the marriage of Lieutenant Boulter and Alice Irene Toone, the bridegroom was residing at Staun House, a residential hotel at 54 & 55 Tavistock Square, Bloomsbury, London WC1. Miss Toone was living at Wigston Hall, the home of her late father, with her half-sister Mrs Edith Birkett and her husband Thomas Birkett. She was known, affectionately, within the family as Rene.

Wigston Hall, Wigston Magna (Duncan Lucas)

Wigston Hall was built in 1834 for Captain Charles Holland Baddeley of the East India Company. It was eventually demolished in 1961.

The marriage took place on Thursday, 14 April 1927 at the St Giles' Register Office, 14-18 Bloomsbury Street, Holborn, London and was reported in the *Kettering Evening Telegraph* under the headlines:

KETTERING'S FIRST VC MARRIED TODAY

Lieutenant Boulter weds Miss Toone

London Ceremony

Alice Irene Toone with her father Benjamin circa 1907 (Jeremy Birkett)

The report described how: "The romance had its beginnings during meetings at Wigston and Leicester". William was 34 years of age and Alice Irene was 29 years at the time of their marriage. The witnesses to their wedding were Billy's parents Fred and Mary Boulter together with Edith and Thomas Birkett.

Lieutenant William Ewart Boulter VC and his bride Alice Irene Toone outside St Giles' Register Office following their wedding on 14 April 1927 (Daily Sketch/Associated Newspapers Ltd)

Edith and Thomas Birkett at their home at Wigston Hall (Duncan Lucas)

The wedding was described, in the *Kettering Evening Telegraph,* as "Being of a quiet nature, there were no bridesmaids". The bride, a lady of style and sophistication, "was married in her travelling dress" and certainly looked very attractive in her furs and finery. Billy, for his part, presented a very dapper appearance complete with bowler hat and spats, the very epitome of an officer and gentleman. Even before the wedding photographs were taken he could not resist the temptation to light up a cigarette!

The wedding reception was held at the Coventry Restaurant in Rupert Street and the couple received a large number of wedding gifts from their respective families and friends. The honeymoon was spent in Worthing.

Following their return from honeymoon, Billy Boulter and his bride made their home in London. In September 1928 he applied to join the firm of John Lewis & Co Ltd. His letter of application was received, with interest by the founder and chairman of the great store John Spedan Lewis. In a memorandum to his financial adviser he commented: "You will agree, I think, the letter indicates considerable energy and intelligence".

Unfortunately, for the applicant, there was no suitable vacancy with the firm that could be offered, at that moment in time, but his application was noted on the firm's waiting list for future reference.

The following year, on Saturday 9 November 1929, a further great event took place for holders of the Victoria Cross. A dinner in their honour was given by the British Legion (Royal British Legion from 1971). The Guest of Honour was His Royal Highness The Prince of Wales (later King Edward VIII) as Patron of the British Legion.

The dinner took place in the Royal Gallery at the House of Lords in the splendour of the Palace of Westminster. Leicestershire was well represented by Lieutenant William Ewart Boulter VC, Captain John Cridlan Barrett VC, a house surgeon at the Leicester Royal Infirmary and Corporal William Bees VC a roadman employed by Coalville Urban District Council.

The Palace of Westminster (Derek Seaton)

The dinner was attended by 321 VC holders and the following day they were entertained, with their wives and friends, to a special performance of the play "Journey's End" by Robert Cedric Sherriff, performed in their honour, at the Prince of Wales' Theatre in Coventry Street, London. The programme for the play, which was in three acts, informed the audience: "The scene is laid in a dugout in the British trenches before St Quentin, March 1918".

At the time "Journey's End", which had been written in 1929, was being performed throughout the world in many of the great cities including New York, Melbourne, Paris, Munich and Stockholm.

William Boulter's desire to join the firm of John Lewis & Co Ltd came to fruition when, in July 1933, he was offered employment. He was engaged on an experimental basis binding upon both sides for one month. This was common practice in order to assess an applicant's suitability for employment with the company. His commencing salary was £500 per annum. He obviously made a very good impression and not only remained beyond the trial period of one month but went on to be appointed to the post of Superintendent of the Departments of Shoes and Trunks, at East House in Oxford Street, London, on 28 September 1933.

In 1933 there were two John Lewis buildings in Oxford Street comprising of the East House which concentrated on fashion related merchandise and the West House which sold fabrics, furniture and household goods.

Lieutenant Boulter seized his opportunity and impressed his employers to the extent that he was promoted to Sales Manager with responsibility for several departments in the Oxford Street store.

By April 1934 he had been appointed to Sales Manager at Messrs Lance and Lance Ltd in Weston-super-Mare. Control of this well established and important department store had been acquired by John Lewis & Co Ltd in November 1933. William Boulter assumed responsibility for all ground floor departments there on 11 April.

An item of publicity material, in the form of a delightful line drawing, gives an impression of the firm's premises.

East House, John Lewis & Co Ltd, Oxford Street, London
(John Lewis Partnership Archive Collection)

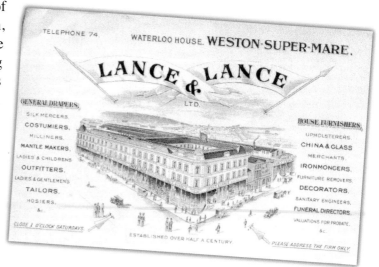

Lance and Lance Ltd, Weston-super-Mare
(John Lewis Partnership Archive Collection)

He returned to Oxford Street later in 1934, moving to West House as Sales Manager of John Lewis' Furnishing Departments. In all of these senior managerial positions he acquitted himself well, gave reviews and reports, of his departments, to John Spedan Lewis and exercised positive leadership to his quite numerous staff. In one report to the Chairman he said of his staff: *"In their technical knowledge, as well as their general personal quality, they are now about as good a team as there is any real scope for, in such a trade as we are doing at present. They are well settled and happy".*

Billy and Rene Boulter were fond of holidays on the south coast. In addition to Worthing, where they spent their honeymoon, Margate was another favourite destination.

A second spell with Lance and Lance Ltd gave

West House, John Lewis & Co Ltd, Oxford Street, London (John Lewis Partnership Archive Collection)

Billy and Rene Boulter on holiday at Margate circa 1934 (Jeremy Birkett)

known for the high quality of its footwear both in terms of its workmanship and the appearance of its products. The firm of B. Toone and Co Ltd was the largest of eight boot and shoe manufacturers in the town and was renowned for its specialised product the "Little Duke" which was the trade name for boots made for boys and youths. The product was advertised as "The aristocrat of Boys' Footwear".

After a short period in Desborough, William Boulter joined the firm of another member of his family. In 1936 he went to work for Knight and Company, auctioneers, surveyors, valuers and estate agents, 14 Cromwell Place, South Kensington, London. The company was owned by Cyril Wilson Black who was married to Dorothy Joyce Birkett the niece of Billy's wife Rene. Cyril Black was a highly successful businessman. A chartered surveyor, he joined his father's property firm of Knight and Company and went on to build a huge property empire and to become a director of over fifty companies.

William Boulter the opportunity to become the firm's Acting General Manager in August 1935 but his time at the Weston-super-Mare store was brief as he only remained at the helm until 20 September that year.

He then moved to Northamptonshire, where he had worked between 1912 and the outbreak of the First World War. On this occasion he joined the firm of Messrs B. Toone and Co Ltd, boot and shoe manufacturers in Desborough. The company had been established by Irene Boulter's grandfather, Benjamin Toone senior and John Wycliffe Black, both from South Wigston in Leicestershire, in the 1860's.

Later the partners separated and the firm was owned by Irene's father Benjamin Toone junior and her half-sister's husband Thomas Birkett. By 1912 the firm was under the control of Thomas Birkett who had the title of 'Governing Director'.

Desborough, situated between Kettering and Market Harborough in Leicestershire, was well-

Cyril Wilson Black (Jeremy Birkett)

This latest appointment was another challenge for Billy Boulter. The management of a variety of properties called for a range of skills, including diplomacy and rapid decision making and here, once again, he embarked upon a new career to which he was able to adapt successfully.

Together with Rene he moved into a new home, an elegant, well-appointed flat at 10 Wimbledon Close, The Downs, Wimbledon in 1936. Life in Wimbledon for Billy and Rene Boulter was tranquil and, although they had no children, they had a wide circle of friends and acquaintances. Both were sociable and outgoing and their easy, relaxed companionship was welcomed by family and friends.

Billy and Rene Boulter outside of their flat at 10 Wimbledon Close (Jeremy Birkett)

Early in 1937, Fred Boulter retired from his position as manager of Wigston Co-operative Hosiers Ltd (the name of the firm had been changed from Wigston Hosiery Society in 1930).

At a social evening held in his honour, he was presented with a gold watch as a mark of esteem and in recognition of his long and valued period of service. The presentation, on behalf of the Committee, was made by one of the firm's oldest employees Miss C. Hurst.

Fred Boulter (3rd from right) on the occasion of his retirement receiving his gold watch from Miss C. Hurst (Midlands Co-operative Society Limited)

Fred Boulter's involvement with the Wigston Hosiers had commenced in 1897 with the birth of the society, and covered a period of forty years of which he had served as manager for twenty-nine years.

An elegant Rene and Billy, in his sartorial best, on the occasion of Robert and Joan Birkett's marriage in Leicester (Jeremy Birkett)

1937 was the year of the Coronation of His Majesty King George V1. A proud Lieutenant Boulter was the recipient of the Coronation Medal to add to his four medals gained in the First World War.

Contact was maintained with their respective families in Leicestershire. On 9 April 1938, Billy and Rene attended the wedding of Rene's nephew Robert Birkett to Joan Shuff at St Philip's Anglican Church, Leicester.

Lieutenant Boulter's military links continued unabated. He regularly attended the annual parade of The Ypres League which took place in London, in November, on Horse Guards Parade. On 4 November 1938 he had the honour of being one of three wreath bearers each of whom was the holder of the Victoria Cross. The three wreath bearers, on that occasion, were:

One of the last photographs taken of Fred Boulter strolling along the sea front at Skegness with his Wife Mary Ann. Skegness was their favourite resort (Mrs Marion Partridge)

Captain Douglas Walter Belcher VC,
1/5th (City of London) Battalion
The London Regiment

Lieutenant William Ewart Boulter VC,
6th Battalion,
The Northamptonshire Regiment

Lance-Corporal Alfred Wilcox VC,
2/4th Battalion,
The Oxfordshire and Buckinghamshire
Light Infantry

On 24 March 1940, Fred the head of the Boulter family died, at the age of 73 years, at his home 65 Central Avenue, Wigston Magna, Leicestershire. His passing was reported in the *Leicester Evening Mail* (27 March 1940) where reference was made to the fact that he began work at the age of ten and earned half-a-crown a week in a local hosiery factory. A self-made man, he helped to form the Wigston Hosiery Society in 1897 and was, for 29 years, the highly successful manager of its factory.

Fred Boulter's funeral service took place at Wigston Magna Congregational Church, on 28 March, where he and Mary had married almost 50 years earlier. In addition to the family mourners, many representatives from Co-operative organisations were present to pay their respects to a pioneer who was described as: "One of the best known Co-operators in Leicestershire". He had gone on to hold the office of President of the Co-operative Productive Federation Ltd and, until shortly before his death, was the Federation's Treasurer, an office he had held for many years. Other organisations represented were the Wigston Bowling Club, the Wigston Conservative Club and Freemasons from the Humberstone (Granite Lodge) of which Fred Boulter was a member.

William Boulter had every reason to be proud of his father's achievements in life and to reflect upon his own accomplishments following the First World War. He was astute, adaptable and possessed business acumen like his father before him.

When the Second World War broke out Lieutenant Boulter VC, then aged forty-six years, offered his services without hesitation. By 1941 he was again wearing the King's uniform. He joined the Royal Air Force Volunteer Reserve, and on 1 February 1941, became Acting Pilot Officer (No 62809) in the RAFVR Training Branch. Promotion to Pilot Officer followed on 1 February 1942 and by late 1942 he had reached the rank of

William Ewart Boulter VC c.1942 (Jeremy Birkett)

Flight-Lieutenant and had assumed command of the Air Training Corps Squadron in Wimbledon.

Although Flight-Lieutenant William Boulter was approaching his 50th year by this time, his sense of duty had in no way diminished and the portrait (c.1942) characterised the steely, determined expression of a "Steelback" serving his country once more.

His employer Cyril Wilson Black also joined the Air Training Corps and became a Flying Officer with the Wimbledon Squadron. Although he had increasingly wide business interests including the onerous responsibility of being Chairman of the Temperance Permanent Building Society he still found the time to serve as an officer in the Air Training Corps. On occasions when there was an evening parade, in a hall in Wimbledon, he would send out his secretary to buy a quantity of buns which would be placed in filing trays, in his car, for him to take along for the

Squadron Leader John Dering Nettleton VC (left) with Flight-Lieutenant William Ewart Boulter VC (right) (Daily Sketch/Associated Newspapers Ltd)

cadets. The young boys who joined the Wimbledon Air Training Corps were well served, in more ways than one, by their officers Flight-Lieutenant William Ewart Boulter VC and Flying Officer Cyril Wilson Black.

On 12 May 1942 Flight-Lieutenant Boulter was outside of Buckingham Palace wearing his RAFVR uniform. Hurrying out of the Palace after being decorated with the Victoria Cross, was Squadron Leader John Dering Nettleton VC, of 44 Squadron, Royal Air Force, the twenty-four year old hero of the Augsberg raid on Germany on 17 April 1942.

In a report in the *Daily Herald* (14 May 1942) the reporter described how the newly decorated Squadron Leader: "Bumped into a middle aged Flight-Lieutenant of the Air Training Corps". After both had apologised they then grinned as they noticed that each of them was wearing the crimson ribbon of the Victoria Cross. They immediately struck up a conversation and posed for photographs to oblige the representatives of the press.

Flight-Lieutenant Boulter found it necessary to

resign his commission, in the Royal Air Force Volunteer Reserve, on 25 July 1944 owing to ill health. He had served for almost 3½ years and was nearing his 52nd birthday.

Following the end of the Second World War, a Victory Parade was held in London Saturday 8 June 1946. Lieutenant Boulter was present at the parade which set off from Regent's Park and marched through the capital to The Mall where His Majesty King George VI took the salute. Remarkably, the King stood with his hand at the salute continuously for 1 hour and 48 minutes as the great parade, led by Field Marshall Bernard Law Montgomery, passed.

In the evening, following the parade, A Victory Day Celebration Dinner and Reception for holders of the Victoria Cross was held at the Dorchester Hotel, Park Lane in central London. Lieutenant William Boulter VC was among the honoured guests at the prestigious dinner which was generously hosted by *The News of the World*. In the following day's edition of the newspaper a list, of all the VC holders who attended, was published.

The Dorchester Hotel, Park Lane, London (Derek Seaton)

William Boulter could reflect, with pride, upon his service during the Second World War. He had made his contribution and many young air cadets would have gained confidence and inspiration from their legendary commander during the wartime years.

Billy and Rene in the garden of their Wimbledon home (Jeremy Birkett)

By this time Billy and Rene Boulter were well established in Wimbledon where life, within easy reach of London, was agreeable and suited them ideally.

They maintained close contact with their roots in Wigston Magna. Billy always visited his brothers and sisters at Christmas time bringing gifts for his family. He also continued to keep in touch with his many friends and former colleagues in Kettering. At a visit to the Kettering Industrial Co-operative Society Ltd in the early 1950s he went around the store shaking hands with everyone. For some it was the first opportunity to meet Lieutenant William Ewart Boulter VC who had earlier worked in the store there.

His youngest brother Harold had also achieved success in his chosen profession having become a buyer for the Co-operative grocery shops in the 1940's. Harold Boulter operated from an office in the warehouse of the Wigston Co-operative Society Ltd in Central Avenue, Wigston Magna, and was a member of the Society's Board.

The departmental store, warehouse and offices of the Wigston Co-operative Society Ltd in Long Street and Central Avenue, Wigston Magna (Derek Seaton)

One important task William Boulter assumed responsibility for, on behalf of Knight and Company, after the war, was acquiring furniture for the many furnished flats the company managed. As a property company the firm managed a range of properties on behalf of several companies on whose boards Cyril Black sat. London had a huge shortage of furnished properties due to both bomb damage and the fact that the government had requisitioned a great deal of property. As they began to release flats back onto the market, Knight and Company's clients would acquire them and contract the company to decorate, furnish and manage the properties.

Billy Boulter was kept extremely busy in the early post-war years seeking out and obtaining furniture. This necessitated him contacting the large furniture retailers in London and representing his firm at property auctions. Undoubtedly, the experience he had gained with John Lewis & Co Ltd, as the firm's Sales Manager of its West House, Oxford Street, Furnishing Departments in the 1930s, together with the range of contacts he had established, made him ideally suitable for the task.

He went on to become a successful businessman in property management and acted as a company director for several prominent firms. In business matters he was very much his father's son. A lover of sport throughout his life, Billy Boulter, despite health problems (going back the trenches of the Somme) always wished to participate in sporting activities. Golf became his passion in the latter stages of his life. He became a member of the Malden Golf Club and in 1950 he was the captain of the Golf Society. The competitive urge remained and he won trophies in 1951 and 1952.

The Clubhouse (built in 1925) Malden Golf Club, Surrey (Derek Seaton)

In 1953 Lieutenant Boulter was accorded an honour which filled him with immense pride and satisfaction when he became President of the 6th Battalion Association of The Northamptonshire Regiment. He had been a keen and active supporter of the Association for many years and to become its President was, for him, the supreme accolade.

A further honour to come his way in 1953 was the award of the Elizabeth II Coronation Medal. He then proudly possessed medals bearing the heads of three sovereigns – King George V, King George VI and Queen Elizabeth II.

The Queen Elizabeth II Coronation Medal 1953 (Jeremy Birkett)

By 1954 Billy Boulter's health was in serious decline, he had taken early retirement due to repeated physical problems and bouts of illness. He was suffering from headaches, generally feeling unwell and found it increasingly difficult to receive guests. His condition progressively deteriorated and he was found to be suffering from a terminal illness.

After a long and painful illness, Lieutenant William Ewart Boulter VC died peacefully at his home 10 Wimbledon Close, The Downs, Wimbledon on Wednesday 1 June 1955 aged 62 years. The cause of death was certified as carcinoma of lungs. His occupation, on the death certificate, was described as:

Estate Agents
Property Manager
V.C.

A generous tribute to William Boulter appeared in the *Wimbledon News* on 10 June 1955 with a front page headline which read: VC ADVANCED ALONE. The report referred to the action in which he was awarded the Victoria Cross and quoted from the official citation in *The London Gazette*.

The funeral took place at Putney Vale Cemetery, some three miles from the Boulters' home in Wimbledon, on Monday 6 June. As a mark of respect and the esteem in which he was held, Lieutenant Boulter's funeral service was attended by the Mayor and Mayoress of Wimbledon, Alderman and Mrs Alick Withall who represented the Borough. Among the family mourners were Alderman Cyril Wilson Black M.P., his former employer who had been elected Member of Parliament for Wimbledon in 1950 and Mrs Dorothy Joyce Black (Rene's niece).

Putney Vale Cemetery Kingston Road, London SW15 (Derek Seaton)

The chapels and offices were erected by the Putney Burial Board in 1890. The builders were Messrs S. & W. Pattinson.

Old comrades from the 6th (Service) Battalion of "The Steelbacks" came led by Brigadier John Lingham, CB, DSO, MC, who represented the Colonel of the Regiment and The Northamptonshire Regiment. A distinguished and highly decorated officer, Brigadier Lingham joined The Northamptonshire Regiment, a year after Lieutenant Boulter, in 1915 and was awarded the Military Cross in 1916. He served for the remainder of the First World War and for the entire period of the Second World War during which he

was awarded the Distinguished Service Order in 1944. Such was the pride felt by the Northamptons for their first winner of the Victoria Cross, from the ranks, in the First World War.

Following cremation, William Boulter's ashes were scattered between two cherry trees, in front of the lily pond, opposite the East Lodge of the cemetery.

A tribute was paid to Lieutenant Boulter in *The Northamptonshire Regiment Journal* (No 3 issued in September 1955). The entire citation published in *The London Gazette* (24 October 1916) was recorded. Reference was made to his keen support of the 6th Battalion Association and that he had been the President of the Association. Details were also given of the representation of the Regiment, at his funeral by Brigadier John Lingham.

William Boulter's last Will and Testament, dated 23 October 1950, in which he was described as a Company Director bequeathed his entire estate to his wife Alice Irene Boulter. The estate amounted to £6917-1s-1d gross with a net value of £6553-6s-10d and probate was granted to his widow by the Registrar, in the High Court of Justice (the Principal Probate Registery) on 21 September 1955.

Rene Boulter continued to live at 10 Wimbledon Close, The Downs for the next thirty-two years. She remained in close contact with members of her family. Her niece Mrs Dorothy

Rene Boulter on the harbour front at St Helier, Jersey (Jeremy Birkett)

Joyce Black became Lady Black in 1959 following the knighthood bestowed upon her husband Cyril. Billy's old boss had also been the Chairman of Surrey County Council (1956-1959) and had received the Freedom of the Borough of Wimbledon in 1957.

Her great loves, during her long widowhood were the family and London. Regular visits to the metropolis would include seeing plays and the shows on the West End and enjoyable evenings, spent with her constant companion Lady Joyce Black, attending concerts at the Royal Albert Hall. Rene, a lady of refinement, would dine at stylish restaurants in London, her favourite being The Ivy (Wheelers) 1 & 3 West Street, Cambridge Circus. Back in Wimbledon she and Joyce would enjoy taking morning coffee together in Elys (Wimbledon) Ltd, departmental store, 22-26 Wimbledon Hill Road.

Holidays too with various members of her family were important to her. Rene particularly enjoyed holidays in the Channel Islands, she loved Jersey for its clear sea air and calm pace of life compared to London.

Rene Boulter with her great-nephew Jeremy Birkett on holiday in Jersey early 1980s (Jeremy Birkett)

Entertaining members of the family was high on her list of priorities and she would prepare and cook magnificent meals for her relatives from Leicester and, subsequently, from Northampton-shire. Significantly she would always insist upon her visitors washing up afterwards!

During her long widowhood, Rene Boulter was able to pass on sound advice to members of her family. She too had business experience having served, with Billy, on the board of one of Cyril Black's hotels - the White Hermitage in Bournemouth.

Alice Irene Boulter, died on 20 January 1988 at The Royal Marsden Hospital, Fulham Road, London, after a short illness, in her 91st year. Her cremation was a private one with family flowers only. The announcement of her death in the local newspaper, specified that donations, where desired, should go to The Royal Marsden Hospital.

Later that year Billy Boulter's dearest wish that his medals should be returned to his Regiment came to fruition. His Victoria Cross plus his three other medals from the First World War, together with the George VI Coronation Medal, were earmarked for the Regimental Museum of The Northamptonshire Regiment by the terms of Rene's will. The Elizabeth II Coronation Medal remained in the possession of his family. Rene's relatives and the Northamptonshire Regimental Association combined to plan a ceremonial handing over of the medals which turned out to be a spectacular occasion in Northampton.

On Sunday 3 July 1988, at 10.30am, a parade of 220 comrades from the Regimental Association marched from Gibraltar Barracks under the command of Lieutenant-Colonel Peter Worthy. The Band and Drums of the 5th (Volunteer) Battalion, The Royal Anglian Regiment led the parade into the centre of the town to the Church of the Holy Sepulchre. Upon the arrival of the Colonel of The Royal Anglian Regiment, General Sir John Akehurst KCB, CBE the parade came to attention and greeted him with a General Salute.

Following his inspection of the comrades, General Akehurst, who was also the President of the Northamptonshire Regimental Association, formally received the set of five medals from Mr Peter Birkett, a nephew of Lieutenant Boulter.

Peter Birkett displaying Lieutenant Boulter's Victoria Cross and other medals at the parade (Jeremy Birkett)

General Sir John Akehurst, Colonel of The Royal Anglian Regiment receiving Lieutenant Boulter's medals from Peter Birkett (Jeremy Birkett)

General Akehurst, displaying the medals to the drawn up ranks of the comrades, then said:

"The Victoria Cross in the most historic, the most famous, the most exclusive and the most prized award for heroism in the world. With typical British understatement it bears only two words FOR VALOUR but it is only given for deeds of spectacular heroism in action. The Victoria Cross we have just received was won by Sergeant, later Lieutenant W.E. (Billy) Boulter in the terrible battle of the Somme."

General Akehurst then read out the full citation and concluded his remarks by informing the assembled ranks:

"Billy Boulter joined the Regiment for the duration of the First World War and thus became part of the family of the Regiment. He always wished that his medals should return to that family and it is his own family who have brought them here to be presented today. We receive them with great pride and they will be placed on display in our Regimental Museum for many thousands of visitors to see in future years".

The medals were then handed to an escort of Warrant Officers from the 2nd, 5th and 7th Battalions commanded by Major Alan W.M. Petch MBE, TD

and taken by the escort into the Church of the Holy Sepulchre, where the Comrades filed in to view them.

Later the medals were placed on display at Simpson Barracks in Northampton during the Officers' Lunch Party at which Peter Birkett and other members of the Boulter family were guests. Sadly, Billy's sister Mrs Sarah May Clarke, living in Haywards Heath, was unable to attend. She was 84 years of age and in poor health but was very interested in the event and arrangements were made for photographs of the presentation to be sent to her.

The honour of receiving Lieutenant Boulter's Victoria Cross and other medals that day was a matter of enormous pride to General Sir John Akehurst. A fellow "Steelback" he had been commissioned into The Northamptonshire Regiment in 1949. He was appointed Adjutant of the 5th Battalion (TA) of his regiment in 1959. In 1968 he was appointed Commanding Officer of the 2nd Battalion of The Royal Anglian Regiment. Ultimately, this remarkable officer progressed to the rank of General.

At the time he received Lieutenant Boulter's medals he was Deputy Supreme Allied Commander, Europe. Thus Billy Boulter, a legendary hero of The Northamptonshire Regiment, was honoured by one of the Regiment's most famous soldiers.

Chapter Six - Reminders

Billy Boulter would not have expected to be remembered after his death but in addition to his proud descendants and military men of Northamptonshire, to whom he was a legend, he is remembered on a wider stage. There are a number of important reminders to be seen which he himself would have considered to be inexplicable to a former soldier who had merely "done his duty".

Each year thousands of visitors are attracted to the delightful Abington Park Museum in Northampton. Set in a public park, Abington houses displays of the town's social history as well as the history of The Northamptonshire Regiment and The Northamptonshire Yeomanry. Appropriately, Lieutenant Boulter's Victoria Cross, together with his other medals remain on permanent display for all to see,

Abington Park Museum, Northampton a Grade I Listed Building (Derek Seaton)

The Victoria Cross (reverse side) awarded to William Ewart Boulter - 14 July 1916 (Jeremy Birkett)

The Record Office for Leicestershire, Leicester and Rutland, Long Street, Wigston Magna, to the right is the Boys' Entrance to the former school (Derek Seaton)

On 13 May 1993, His Royal Highness The Duke of Gloucester GCVO, formally opened the new Leicestershire Record Office in Long Street, Wigston Magna. The former Board School was the one attended by the young Billy Boulter and it was a happy coincidence that it should have been opened by The Duke of Gloucester whose mother Her Royal Highness Princess Alice, Duchess of Gloucester GCB, CI, GCVO, GBE was a former Colonel-in-Chief of The Northamptonshire Regiment.

In 1960 the 1st Battalion, The Northamptonshire Regiment amalgamated with The Royal Lincolnshire Regiment to form The 2nd East Anglian Regiment (1960-1964). Today, His Royal Highness The Duke of Gloucester KG, GCVO is the Colonel-in-Chief of The Royal Anglian Regiment where the spirit and traditions of "The Steelbacks" live on in the 2nd Battalion's C Company (Northamptonshire and Rutland) and the 3rd Battalion (The Steelbacks).

Appropriately, researchers can now visit Billy Boulter's old school where he spent his formative years. It was there that he acquired both educational grounding and a love of sporting pursuits which were to stand him in good stead in the years ahead.

In 1997 Wandsworth Borough Council, conscious of the fact that Putney Vale Cemetery was the resting place of six holders of the Victoria Cross, with a memorial to honour a seventh, took the decision to name seven of the main roads and paths after the VC holders who had been buried, cremated or commemorated there. The resolution also served the purpose of making it more convenient for visitors to find their way around the large 50 acre cemetery.

The pathways, with vehicle access, uniquely named in honour of the seven holders of the Victoria Cross were:

Alexander Way
(Major, later Major-General, Ernest Wright
Alexander, VC, CB, CMG
119th Battery, Royal Field Artillery
Elouges, Belgium 24 August 1914)

Boulter's Path, Putney Vale Cemetery (Derek Seaton)

Boulter's Path
(Sergeant, later Lieutenant, William Ewart
Boulter VC, 6th (Service) Battalion, The
Northamptonshire Regiment
Trones Wood, France 14 July 1916)

Greenwood Road
(Acting Lieutenant-Colonel Harry Greenwood
VC, DSO and Bar, OBE, MC
9th Battalion, The King's Own Yorkshire Light
Infantry
Ovillers, France 23 October 1918)

Hayward Avenue
(Acting Captain, later Lieutenant-Colonel,
Reginald Frederick
Johnson Hayward, VC, MC and Bar
1st Battalion, The Wiltshire Regiment
Fremicourt, France 21/22 March 1918)

Paton's Path
(Acting Captain, George Henry Tatham Paton,
VC, MC
4th Battalion, The Grenadier Guards
Gonnelieu, France 1 December 1917)

Richard's Way
(Sergeant Alfred Joseph Richards, VC
1st Battalion, The Lancashire Fusiliers
Cape Helles, Gallipoli, Turkey 25 April 1915)

Schofield Road
(Captain, later Lieutenant-Colonel, Harry Norton
Schofield, VC
Royal Field Artillery
Colenso, South Africa 15 December 1899)

Always the sportsman, Billy Boulter's latter years brought joy, friendship and a sense of achievement on the golf course. His membership of Malden Golf Club had given him a new opportunity to compete and to socialise, two qualities he possessed in abundance. He was fondly remembered, many years after his death by the club members.

In due course a wonderful tribute in the form of a framed wall-mounting was presented by J.C.S. Pascall, the Captain of Malden Golf Club 2003-04 and hangs proudly in the members' bar. It shows

Malden Golf Club, Surrey
(By kind permission of Malden Golf Club)

two pictures of Sergeant William Ewart Boulter (as he then was) – Edgar A Holloway's painting of him attacking the German machine-gun post in Trones Wood, and the Gallaher Ltd cigarette card portrayal of Sergeant Boulter which featured in the Series of VC Heroes 1916. The pictures compliment his VC citation and set of replicas of his medals and form an impressive token of respect and affection for one of the club's most notable members.

The Blue Plaque to commemorate William Ewart Boulter VC, 9 Central Avenue, Wigston Magna (Wigston Civic Society and Greater Wigston Historical Society)

The wall-mounting to commemorate
William Ewart Boulter VC
(By kind permission of Malden Golf Club) (Derek Seaton)

The memory of William Boulter was further honoured in 2007 in his home village of Wigston Magna. A joint project by the Wigston Civic Society and the Greater Wigston Historical Society to initiate a Blue Plaque scheme, in Wigston Magna and South Wigston, was launched in 2003. The project was designed to commemorate eminent citizens, of local and national importance, connected with the district. Following a successful bid to the Awards for All section of the National Lottery, and a great deal of hard work by a working group from the two societies, the scheme went ahead. Fourteen plaques were subsequently unveiled.

Plaque No 8 honoured Wigston Magna's only holder of the Victoria Cross, Sergeant William Ewart Boulter. It was placed on the front elevation of 9 Central Avenue where the Boulter family lived during the First World War and where, on 26 October 1916, Billy Boulter received the news that he had been awarded the world's most prestigious prize for gallantry.

A splendid booklet, written by Tricia Berry, was published by the two societies in 2007, giving details plus photographs and illustrations relating to the fourteen local people commemorated by the plaques.

Visitors to the battlefields of the Western Front are continually drawn to the area of the Somme where the terrible battles of 1916 left their mark upon the world. For those who go on the conducted tours around the Longueval sector, a visit to the various woods, including Trones Wood, and the nearby memorials convey the sheer scale of the operations and the intensity of the fighting.

Trones Wood, France 2009 (Derek Seaton)

Now completely grown again and looking rather dark and forbidding is Trones Wood where, on 14 July 1916, Sergeant William Ewart Boulter VC encountered what was to prove to be the defining moment in his life.

Appendix I

Officers, NCOs and Men of The Northamptonshire Regiment who were awarded the Victoria Cross in the First World War

Captain Anketell Moutray Read VC
1st Battalion
25 September 1915
near Hulluch, France

Sergeant (later Lieutenant) **William Boulter VC**
6th (Service) Battalion
14 July 1916
Trones Wood, France

Lance-Corporal Leonard Allan Lewis VC
6th (Service) Battalion
18 and 21 September 1916
Rossnoy, near Lempire, France

**Acting Captain Thomas Riversdale
Colyer-Ferguson VC**
2nd Battalion
31 July 1917
Bellewaarde, Belgium

**Temporary 2nd Lieutenant (later Major)
Alfred Cecil Herring VC**
Royal Army Service Corps
Attached to the 6th
 (Service) Battalion
23-24 March 1918
Montagne Bridge, France

**Temporary Lieutenant Frederick
William Hedges VC**
The Bedfordshire
Regiment attached to the 6th (Service) Battalion
24 October 1918
Bousies, France

The Crest of The Northamptonshire Regiment (by kind permission of The Royal Anglian Regiment Association)

The Northamptonshire Regiment gained 9 Victoria Crosses during their glorious history and distinguished service to the Crown.

Appendix II
The Fighting Boulters
One family's response to the Call to Arms

P/J75666
Able Seaman George Boulter
Royal Navy

23766 Private Albert Boulter
2nd Battalion, The Leicestershire Regiment

2nd Lieutenant William
Ewart Boulter VC
6th & 7th (Service) Battalions,
The Northamptonshire Regiment
(Jeremy Birkett)

103331 Private Harold Boulter
Royal Army Medical Corps

The Boulter brothers served in the following areas
of the world between 1914-1919: Belgium,
France, India, Mesopotamia, Russia, Scapa Flow

Appendix III

The Battlefield areas of the Western Front

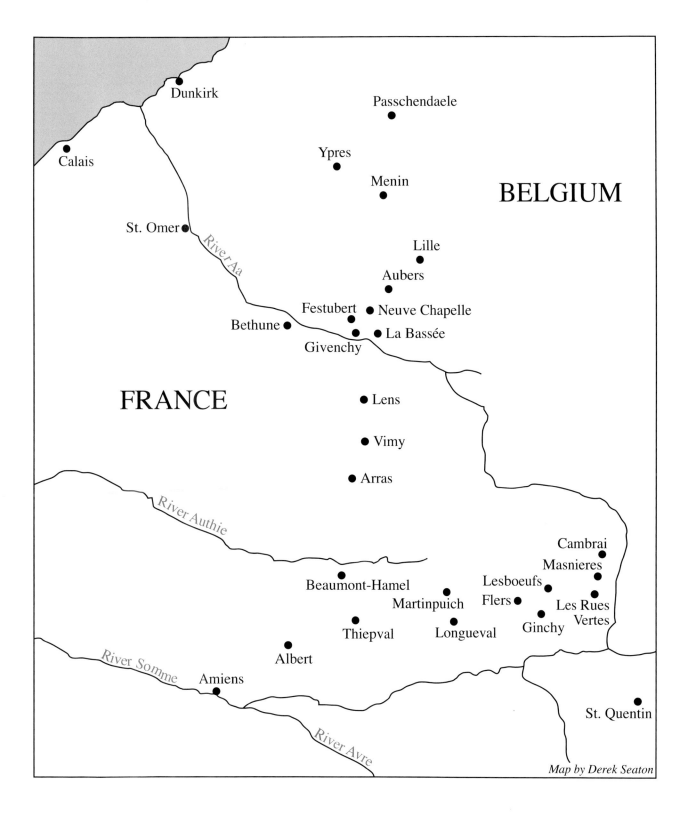

Map by Derek Seaton

Appendix IV
The Bazentin Ridge and Trones Wood

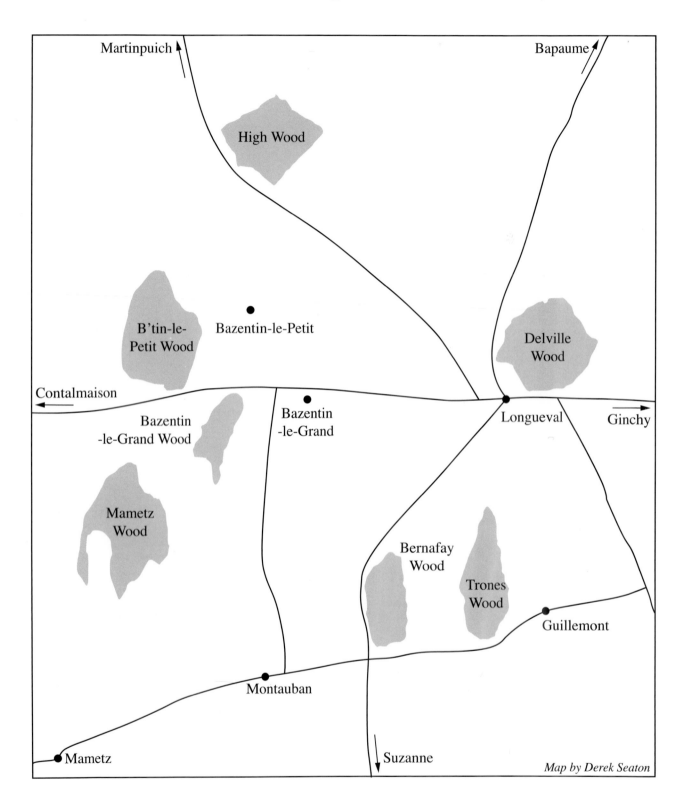

Martinpuich

Bapaume

High Wood

B'tin-le-Petit Wood

Bazentin-le-Petit

Delville Wood

Contalmaison

Bazentin -le-Grand Wood

Bazentin -le-Grand

Longueval

Ginchy

Mametz Wood

Bernafay Wood

Trones Wood

Guillemont

Montauban

Suzanne

Map by Derek Seaton

Mametz

Bibliography

Arthur, Max	*Symbol of Courage: A History of the Victoria Cross*	London	2004
Baynes, John	*Far From A Donkey; The Life of General Sir Ivor Maxse*	London	1995
Berry, Tricia	*Blue Plaques in Wigston Magna and South Wigston*	Wigston	2007
Creagh, General Sir Garrett O'Moore VC & Humphris, E.M.	*The Victoria Cross and The Distinguished Service Order*	London	1924
Duffy, Christopher	*Through German Eyes: The British & The Somme 1916*	London	2006
Gliddon, Gerald	*VCs of the Somme: A Biographical Portrait*	Norwich	1991
Greening, Edward Owen	*A Democratic Co-partnership*	Leicester	1921
Haythornthwaite, Philip, J	*The World War One Source Book*	London	1998
Holloway, William Henry, OBE	*Northamptonshire and The Great War 1914-1918*	Northampton	1922
Holmes, Richard	*The Western Front*	London	1999
Hoskins, William George	*The Midland Peasant*	London	1965
Hunt, Derek	*Valour Beyond All Praise: Harry Greenwood VC*	Windsor	2003
Hunt, Derek and Mulholland John	*A Party Fit for Heroes*	Uckfield East Sussex	2007
Jackson, Peter	*The Glorious Sixth*	Northampton	1975
King, H.B. MC	*7th (Service) Battalion, Northamptonshire Regiment 1914-1919*	Aldershot	1919
Lucas, Duncan, Berry, Tricia and Mastin, Peter	*Wigston Magna and South*	Stroud	1997

Bibliography

Moore, Geoffrey	*Four VCs in Forty Months: The Proud Record in World War I of the 6th (Service) Battalion, The Northamptonshire Regiment*	Buckden, Huntingdon	1981
Rawson, Andrew	*British Army Handbook 1914-1918*	Stroud	2006
Roberts, William V	*A Half-Century of Co-operative Co-partnership 1899-1949*	Leicester	1949
Sheffield, Gary and Bourne, John	*Douglas Haig: War Diaries & Letters 1914-1918*	London	2005
Taylor, Edna and Wignall, John Robert	*For The Record: The story of Long Street School, Wigston*	Wigston	1992
This England	*The Register of the Victoria Cross (Third Edition)*	Cheltenham	1997
Westlake, Ray	*Tracing British Battalions On The Somme*	Barnsley	2009
Woodall, David	*The Mobbs' Own, The 7th Battalion, The Northamptonshire Regiment 1914-1918*	Spratton, Northants	1994

Newspapers

Daily Herald
Daily Sketch
Illustrated Leicester Chronicle
Kettering Evening Telegraph
Leicester Daily Mercury
Leicester Daily Post
Leicester Evening Mail

Leicester Mercury
Northampton Mercury
The Kettering Leader
The London Gazette
The News of the World
The Northampton Independent
Wimbledon News

Other Sources

Article by Jonathan Porter:	*"Chavasse Farm & Nine VC's (Part 2) William Boulter VC Trones Wood 14 July 1916"*

Published in *The Journal of The Victoria Cross Society* (9th Edition) October 2006

Trones Wood, 13 & 14 July 1916	Extracts from General Sir Ivor Maxse's notes on the Somme Situation as it presented itself on 11 July 1916 (National Army Museum)

Other Sources

War Diaries 6th (Service) Battalion, The Northamptonshire Regiment
War Diaries 7th (Service) Battalion, The Northamptonshire Regiment

Church of The Holy Sepulchre, Northampton
A Guide by S.V.F. Leleux BA

Kelly's Directory of Leicestershire 1922

*Kelly's Directory of Leicestershire and
Rutland* 1888, 1901, 1904, 1912 & 1916

Kelly's Directory of Northamptonshire 1906, 1910 & 1931

Every effort has been made to trace and acknowledge the copyright holders of illustrations used in this book but this has not always proved to be possible. I apologise in advance for any unintentional omission and would invite anyone. who feels that an illustration has been used without permission, to contact the author.

Index

Index

Index

Index

2nd Lieutenant William Ewart Boulter V C
(Reproduced by permission of the Northampton Chronicle & Echo)